Christians Hearing Voices

of related interest

Can't You Hear Them?
The Science and Significance of Hearing Voices
Simon McCarthy-Jones
ISBN 978 1 78592 256 5
eISBN 978 1 78450 541 7

Hearing Voices, Living Fully
Living with the Voices in My Head
Claire Bien
Foreword by Larry Davidson
ISBN 978 1 78592 718 8
eISBN 978 1 78450 322 2

Chaplaincy and Spiritual Care in Mental Health Settings
Edited by Jean Fletcher
Foreword by Professor John Swinton
Afterword by Rev. Canon Dr Margaret Whipp
ISBN 978 1 78592 571 9
eISBN 978 1 78450 981 1

Treating Body and Soul
A Clinicians' Guide to Supporting the Physical, Mental and Spiritual Needs of Their Patients
Edited by Peter Wells
ISBN 978 1 78592 148 3
eISBN 978 1 78450 417 5

Christians Hearing Voices

Affirming Experience and Finding Meaning

Christopher C. H. Cook

Jessica Kingsley Publishers
London and Philadelphia

First published in 2020
by Jessica Kingsley Publishers
73 Collier Street
London N1 9BE, UK
and
400 Market Street, Suite 400
Philadelphia, PA 19106, USA

www.jkp.com

Library of Congress Cataloging in Publication Data
A CIP catalog record for this book is available from the Library of Congress

British Library Cataloguing in Publication Data
A CIP catalogue record for this book is available from the British Library

ISBN 978 1 78592 524 5
eISBN 978 1 78450 913 2

Printed and bound in Great Britain

This book is dedicated to my parents,

Margaret and Cyril,

Remembering them with thanks (Sirach 7.28)

Contents

Contents

Acknowledgements

I would like to thank the many Christians who shared with me their experiences of hearing voices during the course of the research that led to the writing of this book. I wish I could have included all of their stories in this book, but I had to be selective. Those that were not included have been just as important in shaping my thinking and writing as those that were, and I am therefore enormously grateful to all. I am aware that these people all took a step of trust in sharing their experiences with me, not least those who were willing to allow publication. It has been a huge privilege to hear their stories and to discuss them in correspondence and in face-to-face meetings with each and every person concerned.

I would also like to thank all of my colleagues on the Hearing the Voice project at Durham University, from whom I have learned so much, and especially Angela Woods and Victoria Patton. It was in conversation with them, at a meeting of 'Voice Club' one Friday afternoon in the early years of the project, that the idea for this book was born. The work would not have been possible but for generous funding from the Hearing the Voice project by the Wellcome Trust (grant numbers WT098455MA and 108720/Z/15/Z).

I am grateful to Adrian Hughes, Angela Woods and Victoria Patton for reading various portions of the manuscript for this book and for providing me with their generous and helpful comments on it.

My thanks must also go to all the staff involved at JKP, and especially Natalie Watson, with whose help the contract for publication was originally negotiated, and Emily Badger, who has provided friendly and helpful support during the actual writing of the book and subsequent processes leading to publication.

Finally, I am grateful, as always, to my wife, Joy, and to my family, for their support and encouragement along the way.

Acknowledgements

Chapter 1

Introduction

Human life is rich with the clamour of voices. We are social creatures and we like to talk. We are good at talking. We are not always as good at listening to one another, but this is at least partly because we are inundated with voices to listen to. In addition to the people with whom we come into direct contact each day, we are presented with voices in written and recorded media, live broadcasts, telecommunications, and an increasing number of electronic devices that use voice as a means of interaction with the human user. There is a lot to listen to, and we have to be selective and discriminating if we are to make sense of it all. The voices that vie for our attention in the world around us are, however, insignificant in comparison with the voices within.

Mental life, for most of us, is a very verbal affair. We have a capacity to visualize, and much of our thinking is permeated by an affective dimension that colours life with emotions, but it is the inner voice that we hear that provides commentary and content to most of the mental goings on that are the medium for our consciousness. From an early age, children learn to adapt social dialogue to the task of self-awareness. At first vocalized out loud, this speech about ourselves and our world soon becomes internalized and silent. It is also abbreviated. We don't have to think in complete sentences, but we do make good use of words, and we can 'hear' a voice within that we recognize as our own. We can also conduct an inner dialogue, talking to ourselves, or imagining a conversation with another person. We aren't always sure who that other person is. Sometimes a thought enters my head that is 'not mine'. It is mine, of course, in the sense that I know it is a thought in my own mind, but it is not something that I own or identify with. It doesn't 'sound' like me. It is the kind of thing someone else might have said.[1]

This inner life, which is so rich in voices, provides a vitally important means of our awareness of ourselves. Inner speech enables us to get to know ourselves; it facilitates self-reflection. However, it is not completely reliable. Sam Wilkinson and Charles Fernyhough, a philosopher and a psychologist respectively, have suggested that our inner voices might mislead us in two ways: by misrepresenting our own state of mind, and by misidentifying to whom the voice properly belongs.[2] The first of these would seem to be common, the second perhaps less so, but together they present us with a problem – how do I know what my inner voices mean if I can't be sure about what they are saying and whose voices they are?

To take a specific example, let's say that in my mind I hear an angry voice: 'Just who does she think she is?!' This might simply be my own thought in response to something unflattering that someone has just said about me. I am cross. Perhaps I am angry and don't like to admit it. I fear that there is truth in what was said and I know deep down that I should reflect further on it. This is not easy to do. Disowning the angry voice within me – identifying it as belonging to another real or imagined person – may serve a protective function, preserving my self-esteem. This 'other' voice within me gives expression to what I find hard to own within myself.

On the other hand, it may be that I am actually not really angry at all. I believe that what was said about me was true, and I am deeply hurt and ashamed, but not angry. The angry voice is mine, but I have misidentified the underlying mental state that evoked it. This voice also protects my self-esteem, but it misleads me in a different way. It (wrongly) tells me that I am justifiably angry, not that I am deeply ashamed.

1 For a much fuller exploration of all of this, see Fernyhough (2016).

2 Wilkinson and Fernyhough (2018).

The voices within us cannot be taken at face value, but neither should we ignore them. Reflecting on these voices, being mindful of what they say and how they say it, but accepting their unreliability can help us to know ourselves better. Another, and related, feature of inner speech that is crucial here is that our voices may tell us more about what we believe than about what we desire. Our inner voices give us access to a knowledge of what we believe more directly than they do to a knowledge of what we desire. Thus, if my inner voice says 'I want to help the homeless', it tells me that this is what I believe I desire, or perhaps what I desire to desire, rather than (necessarily) what I actually desire. However, inner speech also helps us to be self-reflective, and thus become more self-aware. I can ask myself the question, 'Do I *really* want to help the homeless?' My inner dialogue can enable a degree of objective distance whereby I (the observer) can reflect on how I (me) am doing in practice: 'Actually, when I saw that homeless person yesterday, I crossed the road to avoid them.'[3]

In the context of these voices, within us and around us, it is significant that Christians speak of Jesus as 'the Word' that has come into the world, sent by God. In the Old Testament, the voice of God has creative power, and (in Hebrew) God's creatures are 'words'. In the New Testament, in the prologue to John's Gospel, we are told that in the beginning the Word was with God, and was God. Human beings are spoken into existence by a God who permeates all that he has made. The voice of God is infused into every nook and cranny of creation. From the first chapters of Genesis to the final verses of Revelation, the voice of God is heard by his creatures. In the many intervening pages, we learn just how imperfectly human beings hear this voice, but also how perfectly it finds human form, incarnated in Jesus of Nazareth. The life, death and resurrection of Jesus are together the pivotal event of divine speech, comparable only to creation itself. Hearing the voice of God is not just about listening; it is about how we go about living our lives in light of what God has said in Jesus. It is about how we relate

3 For an in-depth discussion of these issues, see Morin (2018) and Machery (2018).

to God and one another, and about what we do.[4] Listening well is an active affair.

Voices, visions and hallucinations

If there are many voices to hear, they may also take a variety of forms. The general assumption seems to be that voices are either 'in our heads', as thoughts, or else 'out loud', arising from the world around us. In fact, the two kinds of voices are less easy to distinguish than is often imagined. I may hear a thought-like 'voice', and know full well that it is not so much what I have thought as what my mother might have said to me. Another thought may come into my mind and I may be less clear where it came from, but quite sure that it is not the kind of thing I would have thought myself. I may have a 'thought' that I should give up my job and become a missionary and be convinced that it was a thought that God put into my mind. Was this the voice of God – or just a thought?[5]

Sometimes people hear a voice out loud, and turn around only to discover that there is no one there. This may happen once in a lifetime, or it may be a regular event. 'Hearing voices', in this sense, is often associated in the popular imagination with mental illness, but we now know that many people hear voices in this way with no evidence of mental disorder. Such voices may or may not have spiritual or religious significance, but some do. The voice that conveys a call to the mission field may be heard 'out loud'. Does that make it more or less reliable as a means of hearing God?

Psychologists and psychiatrists traditionally refer to the more 'out loud' kind of voice, in the absence of any objective source in the external

---

4 The link between hearing and doing is made in the Gospels in various places, notably in the parable of the sower, where the seed represents those who hear the word in all contexts, but only in the good soil does it bear fruit (Luke 8.4–15). A few verses later in Luke's Gospel, Jesus refers to his mother and his brothers as 'those who hear the word of God and do it' (8.21).

5 See Dein and Cook (2015) for a discussion of such experiences as related by participants in research in a London church. Tanya Luhrmann (2012) has conducted extensive research on experiences of this kind in the Vineyard churches in the USA.

world, as an auditory verbal hallucination (AVH).[6] Hallucinations may be defined as:

> A sensory experience which occurs in the absence of corresponding external stimulation of the relevant sense organ, has a sufficient sense of reality to resemble a veridical perception, over which the subject does not feel s/he has direct and voluntary control, and which occurs in the awake state.[7]

Hallucinations may be experienced in any sensory modality, or in multiple modalities, but the focus of the present book is on a particular kind of auditory hallucination, AVHs. AVHs are auditory hallucinations of voices speaking words. AVHs are 'perception-like' – that is, they sound like hearing something with the ears, but they are not actual perceptions of a real voice that could be heard by anyone else standing nearby. Some kinds of AVHs are quite common, for example in the state between wakefulness and sleep, when falling asleep or waking up. Hearing one's name called, only to turn around and discover that there is no one there, is not unusual, and is not indicative of any kind of psychopathology. The identification of a voice as an AVH thus has no diagnostic significance in itself.[8]

Voices also occur as part of certain kinds of religious experience, and are not infrequently referred to in the Judeo-Christian scriptures. From a conversation with God had by Adam and Eve in the Garden of Eden through to the apocalyptic vision of heaven recorded by John in Revelation, there are biblical accounts of men and women who heard the voice of God, or of angels, or other voices. Notably, Jesus is recorded in the Gospels as having heard a heavenly voice at his baptism and then, immediately afterwards, the voice of Satan in the wilderness. St Paul is recorded by St Luke as having heard a voice on the Damascus road.

---

6 For a fuller and more critical account of this, see Cook (2018, pp.3–8).

7 David (2004, p.110).

8 Certain kinds of AVHs, for example third-person voices talking about the person hearing them, have traditionally been considered diagnostic of schizophrenia. However, it is now clear that the differences between voices diagnosed as pathological and those that are not are less marked than previously thought. For a further discussion of the research, see Cook (2018, pp.3–8).

Subsequently, Christian history has presented many similar accounts, and also some very dissimilar accounts. For example, in the 4th century, St Antony of Egypt can be understood as following the example set by Christ when he also hears the voice of the Devil in the desert. In the early 20th century, the voice that Sundar Singh hears at his conversion is very similar to that heard by St Paul. On the other hand, in the 14th century, Julian of Norwich experienced a series of visions accompanied by voices that, although drawing on biblical content (the passion of Christ), do not appear to be modelled on any particular biblical precedent. Also in the 14th century, Margery Kempe's familiar and ongoing conversations with God and with various saints, although engaging her in dialogue with biblical characters (notably Mary and Jesus), do not seem to emulate any particular biblical pattern of experience.[9]

Of course, we have no way of knowing exactly what kind of experiences Jesus had at his baptism or St Paul had on the Damascus road. Both voices appear to have been heavenly and heard 'out loud'. Technically, they would be AVHs. Christians might argue that they are not hallucinatory, because it was God that was speaking, and God was 'really there'. However, Paul's companions did not hear the voice that he heard. Only in Matthew's Gospel is it clear that the crowd (as well as Jesus) heard the voice when Jesus was baptised. Even then, the voice came from heaven and not from a visible speaker. Referring to such voices as AVHs may appear to be prejudicial, or lacking in faith, but it is, in fact, only a comment concerning the form – or phenomenology – of the experience, according to the definition provided above, and makes no judgement about the reality of the experience or (more crucially) what it means.

If God does speak to people (as Christians have traditionally asserted that he does), what form does that speech take? Is it an 'out loud' voice, or is it more like a thought? In either case, it is presumably not the form of the experience that matters, but rather the content of what was said, and the divine identity of the speaker. Biblical and historical accounts of such experiences, where any relevant information

9 For further details concerning these and other examples from Christian scripture, see Cook (2018), especially Chapters 3, 4 and 5.

is provided, are very variable in form. Recent scientific[10] research into contemporary Christian experiences of hearing God in prayer suggests that Christians hear some voices that are more like thoughts that God put into their minds, and some that are more like voices 'out loud'.[11] In scripture and history, voices have often accompanied visionary experiences. It has been suggested that Protestants hear voices and Catholics see visions, but the evidence for this is debatable.[12]

Not all voices that Christians hear (or visions that they see) necessarily come from God. Evagrius of Pontus, in the 4th century, suggested that our thoughts (we might say our 'inner voices') may be identified as human, angelic or demonic in origin.[13] Sometimes it is not clear who has spoken, and important questions arise concerning discernment. How might a Christian know whether or not it was God whose voice they heard? Similar questions arise in the Bible and in Christian tradition in relation to prophecy.[14]

Generally, in this book, I refer to voices simply as 'voices', making no judgement as to whether they are more thought-like or more perception-like. I leave the participants who have generously shared their stories with me to describe for themselves what their experiences were like. It might be tempting sometimes to label such voices as 'imaginary', or 'hallucinatory', or perhaps as 'mystical' or 'visionary'. They might sound as though they came from God, or they might sound more demonic. It might be tempting to categorize them as inspired or deceptive, but – the question should always be asked – on what grounds might such distinctions meaningfully be made? What should the criteria for discernment be? We shall return to this question in the penultimate chapter of the book. Meanwhile, I propose that the reader should simply listen well and suspend judgement. As author of this book, and as editor of the contributions that I have selected and arranged within it, I shall attempt to do the same.

---

10 I am thinking of science very broadly here, including anthropology and the social sciences.

11 Dein and Cook (2015); Dein and Littlewood (2007); Luhrmann (2012).

12 Cook (2018, p.149).

13 Cook (2011b, pp.31–33).

14 See, for example, Moberly (2006).

How this book came to be written

This work arose as a result of my involvement as a co-investigator in the Wellcome-funded Hearing the Voice project at Durham University.[15] Running from 2012 to 2020, the project has sought to gain a better understanding of the experience of hearing voices that no one else can hear. Such experiences can be deeply distressing, but they can also be very positive and meaningful. We studied such experiences in literary and historical context, and in contemporary experience. The project has been inherently interdisciplinary, including researchers from diverse backgrounds, notably English literature, medieval studies, philosophy, psychology and theology.

My own interest throughout this project has primarily been in the spiritual and religious experiences of voice hearing. However, I have approached the work from an interdisciplinary engagement of my own. Training originally in medicine, then specialising in psychiatry, I worked in mental health services for over 25 years, mainly in addiction psychiatry. During the course of this work I became aware of how upsetting, but also how preoccupying, voices can be in the context of mental ill health. Sometimes these voices had spiritual or religious significance, but often they did not. It has been said that religious voices are declining in frequency in the secular Western world, but a critical review that I conducted of the scientific literature suggests that this is not the case.[16] Spiritual and religious concerns often get mixed up with the psychopathology of mental illness.

I first studied academic theology as an optional course when I was a medical student, but only came back to it later in life, when training for ordination in the Church of England. My experience in the Church, both as a layperson and as a priest, has been that some Christians have a strong sense of what they believe God is saying to them. They are often not specific about exactly what the shape and form of the experience of God speaking to them was like, but they nonetheless have a strong sense of conviction of the importance of it. A variety of popular Christian books have been written on the subject, but many

15 See https://hearingthevoice.org.
16 Cook (2015).

of these have been more concerned with promoting than studying or exploring experiences of 'hearing God'.[17] As I have reflected on such experiences, as people have related them to me over the years, I have become more and more interested in understanding what they mean.

In my earlier years in Durham, I worked on a PhD in theology under the wise supervision of Andrew Louth. Professor Louth introduced me to the rich Orthodox tradition of prayer as explored in depth in an anthology of spiritual writings known as the *Philokalia*. The *Philokalia* has been of huge spiritual importance in the Orthodox East, although still largely unknown to many Western Christians. Its contributors, ranging from the 4th to the 15th centuries, demonstrate a depth of knowledge of how human thoughts reflect, relate to and encounter the Divine, gained from their experiences of prayer. They show very little interest in voices and visions. They are deeply aware of the different sources on which our thoughts draw. They are aware of how easily we deceive ourselves. Amidst, and despite, all of this, they retain a strong sense of the importance and possibility of the human encounter with God.[18]

In this context, as I began the work with the Hearing the Voice project that led to my recent book, *Hearing Voices, Demonic and Divine*,[19] I became fascinated by the different stories that Christians told me of the voices they had heard. At one event, where our research team had met with people with diverse experiences of voice hearing, including one Christian lady who told me about a voice that interrupted her prayers, the idea for the present book was born. I am particularly grateful to my colleagues Victoria Patton and Angela Woods, in conversation with whom the idea of bringing together a collection of such experiences was first floated on that day.

17 One of the best known, and for me most helpful, was Joyce Huggett's *Listening to God* (1986). Also notable, and helpful for its inclusion of stories drawn from the author's pastoral and international experience, is *Does God Speak Today?* by David Pytches (1989). See also Cunningham and Rogers (1984); Praying Medic (2017); Willard (1999); and Williamson (2016).

18 Cook (2011b).

19 Cook (2018).

Science and theology

Experiences of voice hearing, both in clinical groups and in the wider population, have increasingly become the subject of scientific, clinical and interdisciplinary research. There are a variety of scientific theories as to the mechanisms underlying AVHs. The most popular concern the similarities between AVHs and inner speech, and propose that AVHs are internally generated, but misattributed to an external source. However, AVHs are not just thought-like; they are also perception-like. Research on perception reveals that the information about the world around us, as received through our ears or eyes, is ambiguous. So-called 'top-down' processing of this information by the brain makes sense of it in terms of what we expect to hear, or see. Depending on what we give our attention to, and what we expect, we may get things wrong and hear, or see, things that are not actually there. Whichever theory is correct (and I have simplified things here), the underlying common theme is that AVHs (and other hallucinatory experiences, such as visions) arise from within our own minds and brains, based on our own inner speech, thoughts, memories or expectations.[20]

A crude form of scientism might take this research as evidence that there is 'nothing there', and that the meaning of spiritual experiences of AVHs or visions is superimposed after the fact. Thus, human beings create their own meanings. A crude supernaturalism might reject the science out of hand, and assert instead that the visions of Julian of Norwich, or St Paul's encounter with Jesus on the road to Damascus (or similar experiences today) were miraculous. I don't think that either of these approaches is helpful or convincing. Scientists, and clinicians, are increasingly aware that voices can be meaningful and significant, relating back biographically to traumatic (or otherwise significant) memories. The mechanisms by which they arise do not tell us what the visions and voices mean, and nor do they deny the meaningfulness of these experiences. Similarly, theologians are also aware that science, properly interpreted, is not an enemy but a friend. Our expanding knowledge of the created order encourages us to ask important theological questions. Much of this work has focused on

20 For a fuller account, see Cook (2018, pp.175–188).

a limited number of areas of research, such as evolution, quantum physics and cosmology, but the same principle of constructive dialogue between science and theology applies in relation to visions and voices too.[21]

I have proposed elsewhere that some voices may be revelatory. That is, they may be revelatory of God, or they may reveal something important communicated by God.[22] Of course, this begs the question as to how we distinguish between those that are and those that are not revelatory, and I shall return to this towards the end of this book. For now, the important point to make is that science and theology may be seen as friends in this quest, and not as implacable enemies.[23]

Spiritually significant voices

The stories I have included in this book represent the experiences of more than 30 men and women, most of whom responded to a series of three articles that I published in the *Church Times* in 2017.[24] Others were people I met at conferences, or in church, or in other ways. I received relevant material from more than double the number of people actually represented in this book, but there is simply not space here to include them all. As may be expected, I have tried to include representative examples and have attempted to avoid unnecessary duplication. Based on what I received, I do not think that there are any significant forms or types of voices that I have omitted from this anthology. However, the sample is clearly highly selected and may

---

21 For a fuller account, see Cook (2018, pp.189–198).

22 See Cook (2018, pp.199–228).

23 Clearly there is a lot more that could be said about this. The interested reader is referred to Barbour (2002); Hick (2010); and Polkinghorne (1998).

24 Cook (2017a, b, c). The articles were included both in the hard copy of the *Church Times* and online. Each article included a request at the end, indicating that the author would be 'keen to hear from readers who are willing to share their own experiences of hearing spiritually significant voices' and providing contact details. Approval to undertake this work was provided by the Ethics Committee of the Department of Theology and Religion at Durham University.

not be more widely representative of the voices that Christians hear.[25] I would love to hear from anyone who has a different kind of story to share.

The channels through which these stories were collected were primarily Christian, and so, although I only asked for accounts of 'spiritually significant' voices, not specifying any particular religious tradition, it is not surprising that they are all presented within a Christian framework of understanding. They represent a broad cross-section of different Christian traditions, from conservative to liberal, and evangelical to catholic. Not everyone who responded to my request was brought up as a Christian and Lucy's story (see Chapter 7) is particularly interesting in this regard, as she came from a Buddhist background. I would be very pleased to hear from any readers from other faith traditions who may have accounts of experiences of spiritually significant voices they have heard within other religious contexts.

Whilst I do not think that it is only Christians who have experiences of hearing such voices, I do think that Christian experiences share a certain family resemblance, and Christianity seems to have been particularly receptive of voices in certain ways (even if not entirely uncritical). One of the advantages of looking in depth at a particular tradition (in this case, Christianity) is that the voices can more easily be related to their scriptural, historical and theological context, and this is what I have tried to do. It does also appear that voices may be more characteristic of Christianity than of other faith traditions. This appearance may be misleading, and simply a reflection of the fact that much less research has been conducted in respect of other faith traditions. In one cross-cultural study, patients with a diagnosis of schizophrenia in Saudi Arabia were much more likely to have religious

25 This was not, of course, a deliberately selective process, but arose by virtue of the limits and restrictions of the process of ascertainment. The sample is predominantly from the UK, with women slightly over-represented, and with significant numbers of clergy contributors. Given the small sample size, and the non-representative nature of the sample, it is not possible to draw any statistical conclusions.

themes to their voices than similar patients in the UK.[26] However, this does not necessarily extrapolate to religious experience outside the context of mental illness, and we might speculate that religious experiences in other traditions less commonly include the hearing of a voice.

My general approach has been to include first-hand accounts of experiences of voice hearing in people's own words. Having met, or heard from, people who told me that they had heard spiritually significant voices, I asked whether they would be willing to provide me with a written account of their experience(s). Where the reply was in the affirmative, and when I actually received a text describing an experience, or experiences, of voice hearing, there often followed a process of correspondence in which I asked people to clarify anything that was ambiguous, or perhaps to provide further information. Queries were raised, and responded to, in regard to matters that might generally be referred to as 'copy-editing'.[27] This iterative process led to production of a text by each contributor that provided their account of their experience in their own words. These are the texts that I have collected, arranged and introduced in the present book.

I have identified the contributions that I received by first name only. In the great majority of cases, contributors were happy to use their real names. In the exceptional cases where contributors wished to remain anonymous, pseudonyms have been adopted, and this is indicated in each case in a footnote. Although this book arises from my research, I have viewed contributors primarily as authors who have kindly shared their accounts of lived experience with me for inclusion.

I have been conscious of the great privilege of receiving the material that people have sent to me. I do not feel that it is my place to pass judgement on their experiences. I accept what they tell me as their truthful account of what happened, and I have not had reason to doubt the veracity of what I have been told. Similarly, I accept their honest attempts to make sense of it all. Their interpretations of what happened

26 Kent and Wahass (1996).

27 This included attention to grammar, spelling and language as might be expected for any book publication, but always ensuring that the final text accurately reflected the experience of the respondent in their own words.

are just that – their interpretations – and it has been really helpful to me to better understand the different ways in which Christians do interpret their experiences of hearing a voice. I therefore present these stories here, in Chapters 2 to 12, on their own terms. In each chapter, I have provided a brief introduction to how the experiences related might be located within the context of Christian scripture and tradition. At the end of each chapter, I have tried to draw out, where appropriate, some common themes or identify otherwise important matters arising. I have not sought to offer any view on whether my contributors are right or wrong in their interpretations. I do not feel that it is my place to do that.

At the same time, I do recognize that readers will have their own questions about what they read, and perhaps will arrive at different interpretations from those offered by the contributors themselves. Exploration of these different perspectives is part of the reason for writing this book, and I do not want to leave that critical work entirely neglected. However, I also wish to undertake it with due respect to those who have shared their stories with me. I have therefore postponed it until the final two chapters, where I attempt to undertake it in general terms, without prejudice to the views of my contributors and, as much as possible, without reference to their specific stories (except where this may be done affirmingly). In case it is not already completely obvious, the views that I express there are entirely my own.

The aims of writing this book

The first aim of this work is descriptive – there is still much that we do not know about the phenomenology, or subjective form, of Christian experiences of voice hearing. We also do not know a lot about exactly what the voices commonly say. The majority of the voices reported here were perceived as divine, but I have included examples of demonic and other voices, where these were made available to me.

The second aim is my attempt at a taxonomy of the experiences that were shared with me. This is based largely on the content of what the voices said, but it also takes into account the affective quality of the experience, the perceived identity of the voice, the frequency and context of the experience and the quality of the voice. I do not imagine that this taxonomy is the last word on how to classify such experiences, but I hope that it may be a helpful starting point. In particular, I have been struck by the enormous difference between the 'once in a lifetime' experience of a voice associated with conversion, or with a particular vocational calling, and the more everyday conversational experience that some Christians have. Chapters 2 to 6 relate more to the former kind of experience; Chapters 7 to 12 relate more to the latter kind of experience. The majority of experiences shared with me were positive, and Chapters 2 to 9 largely fall into this category. Chapters 10 to 12 include some more unpleasant, complex or difficult experiences. However, there is much overlap between the categories that I have devised, and the taxonomy has been more a convenience for writing the book than a theologically or scientifically satisfactory classification.[28]

My third aim was to explore the important issue of discernment in relation to a collection of first-hand accounts of Christian experiences of voice hearing. I have attempted to address this in Chapter 13.

My fourth, and most important, aim is in Chapter 14, where I explore some of the practical, clinical and pastoral questions that confront mental health professionals, clergy and chaplains. This book is intended to be a guide for them, with a view to avoiding the kinds of misunderstanding that all too often occur when a Christian person says, 'God told me…' I would like to dispel the myths and combat some of the stigma surrounding such experiences. They are far from uncommon. They are not evidence of mental disorder. This does not mean that we must accept them uncritically, but neither does it give us grounds to dismiss them. This book aims to provide a practical and constructive approach to Christian voice hearing.

---

28 In *Hearing Voices, Demonic and Divine* (Cook 2018, p.152), I proposed a slightly different taxonomy of four categories: mystical experience, crisis and transformation, mental illness, and prayer. My approach there emerged from the published literature on religious experience, whereas in the present book I am more concerned with the best categories within which to organize the stories that have been given to me by my contributors. I do not see these differing taxonomies as incompatible, but both are provisional.

Chapter 2

Conversion

The stories of some lives are marked by a turning point around which everything seems to pivot. Such is the significance of these turning points that the rest of life is interpreted in relation to them. The way things were 'before' may be remembered more darkly and the way things have been 'after' recounted more gladly than perhaps the facts may warrant. Yet, there can be no doubt that something deeply significant has changed. Such changes may be marked in behaviour and way of life, in vocation, in values and beliefs, in affections and in social affiliation, but most especially in relation to God.

According to William James, conversion is:

> ...the process, gradual or sudden, by which a self hitherto divided, and consciously wrong inferior and unhappy, becomes unified and consciously right superior and happy, in consequence of its firmer hold upon religious realities.[1]

For James, religion was defined in relation to the divine; as Christians would say, in relation to God. Whilst all Christians might agree that life is better ('consciously right superior and happy') for being lived in relationship with God, not all can identify a discrete turning point that they would call conversion. Within some Christian traditions, notably evangelicalism, more importance has been placed on conversion experiences than in others. However, Christians from diverse cultural and geographical origins, and those who end up in very different parts

1 James (1902, p.189).

of the universal Church, give testimony to such experiences. Countless examples may be cited, from biblical times (and especially in the Book of Acts) down to the present day.

Amongst the most famous early conversation narratives we may note the stories of Paul of Tarsus (formerly known as Saul) and Augustine of Hippo. In very different ways, both were marked by experiences of hearing a voice. Both have been widely influential and have shaped the way in which subsequent conversion stories have been told. It is never possible to completely separate an experience from its context, including the context of the telling and retelling of the conversion stories of others who went before. Augustine himself acknowledges that he was influenced by the story of St Antony of Egypt, written down by Athanasius. Athanasius's *Life of Antony* circulated widely in the early Christian world and made a deep impression on Augustine, as it did on many others. The relating of an experience is also itself part of the experience, so that conversion storytelling is, in an important sense, part of the experience of conversion. We come to better understand our own stories through having had to put them into words and explaining them to another person. Had we not done this, they would have been both different and almost certainly less significant.

The only account that we have now of the conversion of Saul is the one provided to us by Luke. However, having related this to us in the third person in chapter 9 of Acts, Luke has Paul telling and retelling his story in the first person in chapters 22 and 26. Details of the story vary slightly in these three accounts, but in each case the voice, accompanied by a bright light, says 'Saul, Saul, why do you persecute me?'[2] The hearing of these seven words (only five words in Greek) marks the turning point not only for Saul's future life as Paul the Apostle, but also for the future of the whole Christian Church.

Augustine's account of his conversion experience is provided in his *Confessions*. In contrast to Luke's account of Paul's conversion,

2 Acts 9.4; 22.7; 26.14. In the third of these accounts, the voice also goes on to say 'It hurts you to kick against the goads.' In all three accounts Saul responds, 'Who are you Lord?' and the voice then responds to Saul's question, identifying itself as Jesus. The form of words of the response varies slightly in each case.

Augustine tells us much about the processes of thought that precede the actual event. Augustine and Paul shared an antipathy to Christianity prior to their respective conversions, but Augustine relates in detail the process whereby this antipathy transmuted to admiration and then to a struggle with conflicting desires for and against conversion. (Luke gives us no such account of Saul's thinking, so that his conversion is a much more unexpected development in the narrative when it does take place.) Both Paul and Augustine went on to become forceful apologists and evangelists for Christ following their conversions. The voice that marked Augustine's conversion was, however, very different from the one that marked Paul's.

For Augustine, the turning point occurred in a garden in Milan in 386. Hearing the voice of a child chanting in a neighbouring garden, 'Take it and read, take it and read', he took the words as a divine command. Opening the book of scripture that he had to hand, he read from Paul's letter to the Romans (13.13–14):

> ...not in revelling and drunkenness, not in debauchery and licentiousness, not in quarrelling and jealousy. Instead, put on the Lord Jesus Christ, and make no provision for the flesh, to gratify its desires.

Immediately these words seemed to speak to Augustine's predicament and the impact on him was not merely a rational development of the arguments that had been occupying his thoughts for some time previously; rather, it was an emotional experience within which his previous doubts vanished, no longer holding any conviction for him:

> It was as though the light of confidence flooded into my heart and all the darkness of doubt was dispelled.[3]

Of course, not all conversion experiences involve voices in the way that Paul's or Augustine's did. However, some, perhaps many, do. In one of the earliest studies of conversion experiences, Edwin Starbuck provides examples of one woman who heard a voice that said 'Thy sins are forgiven thee; arise go in peace' and a man who heard a voice

3 Augustine's *Confessions* 12.VIII. The translation is from Pine-Coffin (1961).

that said 'There is one, even Christ Jesus, can speak to thy condition.'[4] More recent examples, from a different cultural context, are provided by Joshua Iyadurai.[5] Similar stories may be located in various autobiographical accounts of conversion.[6]

I am pleased to include here two accounts of conversion experiences associated with a voice. Philip's story is associated with a visionary, as well as voice hearing, experience. The account provided here explains something of the context leading up to this experience. In common with the otherwise quite different experiences of Augustine and Antony of Egypt, the reading of a verse of scripture plays a significant part in this story. Whilst this narrative does not go on to relate events after Philip's conversion, it was a life-changing experience, and Philip was later ordained as a priest.

Keith's experience was also life changing, and also took place in a church building, but was much more unexpected. Keith's account focuses more on events following his hearing of the voice, and he has continued to reflect on the significance of the six words that he heard on a particular day, almost 30 years ago. He considers that they have given him purpose in life, although it was, in fact, not about purpose that the voice spoke so much as returning and belonging.

PHILIP'S STORY

I am from a working-class home of fairly mixed origins: English, Irish, Spanish and Jewish being the bits I've tracked down so far. My upbringing was completely non-Church but as with many thousands born at the time (1950) I was baptised at age two months. I never entered a church again until my early twenties.

I became very interested in philosophies from an early age, both religious and political. Apart from a few hymns in assembly at school, and listening to 'Nine Lessons and Carols' on the radio, I had no Christian input from my family, although both my parents were very moral/ethical people.

---

4 Starbuck (1901, pp.79, 87).

5 Iyadurai (2015).

6 I discuss three such examples in Cook (2018, pp.159–161).

I was the first in [the] family to go to university, where I read law. I became quite depressed and homesick, although didn't recognize it as such at the time. I got very involved in the whole drugs, sex and rock'n'roll scene of the late 60s. I once visited the RC [Roman Catholic] chaplaincy, but was mainly impressed with good coffee and nice girls! The chaplain was actually a lovely man.

At [the] end of my second year I gave up on law and started visiting the local student pub at home where I met a chatty group who turned out to be Christians. They invited me to church and I started going occasionally. On Palm Sunday 1972 I attended the church, a Congregational Chapel, for their evening service. It was a Communion service and the text was John 3.1–17. The church was not very full; there were probably a dozen youngish people, including my pub friends.

At the reading of verse 14 I went into a trance-like state and was completely oblivious to my surroundings. Through the 'cloud' I saw the face of Jesus on the cross. He was sweaty, clearly in great pain and anguish and looked me full in the face and said, 'I did this for you.' I gradually emerged from my trance-like state and was crying and said something like, 'I've found God.' I was aware of people staring at me and somebody taking me by the arm to see the minister. He and a youth leader prayed for me, laying hands on me as they did so. I had an overwhelming feeling of joy and happiness. I felt I transcended my own being at that point in time and was in touch with what I called the cosmic reality.

KEITH'S STORY: SIX LIFE-CHANGING WORDS

At the end of 1991, after a life position of atheism since the age of 16, I was 47 when I wandered into our local church (just out of nostalgia, I told myself!) and seemed to be addressed in these words:

> Keith, it's time you came home.

It was a crowded church, full of people and Christmas preparation, not at all 'mystical' or 'spiritual'. The voice certainly seemed to be outside myself. I could hear it but nobody else seemed to. I'd recently felt my certainty about my atheism weakening. So why was I there anyway? Was I setting myself up to 'stage' some epiphany, I wondered in retrospect?

I pondered this event, about which I felt both devastated and suspicious, for months, only telling my wife what had happened, and gradually, tentatively, began to come to church, although aware that what I'd heard could well have been a delusion. I later, after a lot of hard thinking, decided there was no other explanation than that God (however at that stage I conceived of God) had actually spoken to me, that I wasn't deluded or crazy, but that I had been instructed to embark on a new kind of life that had always been my 'home', though unrecognized or resisted. I guess that generalized theism based mainly on intellect, rather than Christian faith, was where I moved to, until over time my commitment deepened, although it was still not well articulated for a long time.

Eventually, around 2003, I took the plunge to train as a reader (lay minister) in the Church of England. I resolved to pay back for the years of unbelief by working each day in the service of God, by preaching, teaching, leading worship, and doing pastoral work in hospital and care homes. Ten years after being licensed, I still do these things.

What have been the long-term effects on me? The experience fades from time to time, although it is regularly renewed by new, if less dramatic, interventions. Usually it happens at the altar rail with a feeling of 'presence', or in moments of silent prayer. If asked, as I am from time to time, how the experience has changed me, I say that becoming a Christian has not made me happier so much as more purposeful.

I have no illusion that the numinous encounter I had makes me in some way better or possessed of extra insights than others. But I do believe that the call I had was genuine, was from God, and was specific to me.

Converting voices

It would not be too difficult to reduce the voices that Paul, Philip, Keith and others have heard to a psychological account that divorces them from transcendent reality and explains away their significance beyond anything other than a resolution of cognitive dissonance or a search for belonging. To do this would do violence to the integrity of the narratives and would be disrespectful of the interpretations that those who heard the voices came to affirm. It was, in any case, not an option that was open to Paul of Tarsus, for whom modern psychological explanations were not available. Had they been, one might imagine that he would have presented a robust defence against them. A reading of his letters (the only texts that he wrote that we now have available to us) makes clear that he had thought deeply about his faith in light of both the religious and philosophical challenges of his time. It would seem unlikely that modern science would have upset his beliefs had he encountered it. But might it have done so?

The voices that mark at least some conversion narratives may indeed reflect subconscious goings on, but this only affirms what we might already have presumed – that conversion is a psychological process as well as a spiritual one. Indeed, whilst it is fairly easy to imagine a psychological conversion of some kind that is not spiritual or religious (for example a conversion to a different political party, or perhaps a conversion of interpersonal human affections), it is difficult to imagine any religious or spiritual conversion devoid of psychological significance. Something as significant as a conversion to Christian faith will, inevitably, have a psychological component to it. As Philip relates it, his experience was one of joy and happiness. As Keith explains, it may not have made the rest of his life happier, but it has given him a sense of purpose.

In our imagined encounter of Paul with the arguments of modern science, we might therefore not expect that a psychological explanation of what happened on the Damascus road would cause him much concern. We might, however, expect that he would have something to say about the 'reality' of his experience of the voice. It was not just a voice; it was Jesus whom he encountered. Indeed, he seems to compare his experience of an encounter with Jesus with the resurrection appearances that took place in the days immediately following the discovery of the empty tomb.[7] The depth of conviction associated with such an encounter is not easily explained away to the satisfaction of the one who has had it, even if it might be explained away to the satisfaction of the sceptical atheist. Indeed, the conviction of the

7 1 Corinthians 15.1–8.

sceptic is in many ways similar to the conviction of the believer. It is this conversion of convictions that is at the heart of what conversion is all about. Whilst it might, at one level, be the case that such convictions are rationally held and defensible, it is also, at another level, something of a mystery as to why we hold them. The psychologist might invoke unconscious – and thus invisible – psychological explanations. The Christian might invoke divine grace. None of this would be likely to dislodge Paul from his Christian convictions.

Chapter 3

Calling

The idea of vocation, or calling,[1] implies the hearing of a voice that calls. In common parlance this voice that calls is now usually taken metaphorically (if it is acknowledged at all), and the emphasis is more on an inner sense of purpose or attraction that draws a man or woman toward a particular occupation, community or way of life. If we might still understand this inner sense of calling as a 'voice', it is usually not verbal until we try to articulate it ourselves. It is more ineffable than that. Most of us discover our vocation as we engage with family, society, education and a wider world that overwhelms us with choice. As we explore the options open to us, we find that some things excite us and give us life. Others are draining and discouraging. We are good at some things, and others give us praise for them, but hardly anyone is good at everything. Our vocation becomes a matter of doing what we are good at, and what we enjoy.

As we get to know ourselves better, and as we learn from the experiences that life bestows upon us, our sense of vocation may change. Famously, in mid-life, some people give up everything in order to change track and pursue something new. Most of these people did not hear a literal voice that told them to do this, but were attentive to the call of their own hearts to something more fulfilling. Of course, this does not mean that they always get it right. It takes a lot of wisdom and self-knowledge to know whether or not this heartfelt longing is realistic, constructive or good.

---

1 Latin: *vocare*.

All Christians share a common baptismal vocation to life in Christ. The nature of this vocation is often presented metaphorically in scripture. Thus, for example, in Luke's Gospel (5.10), Jesus tells Simon Peter, the fisherman, 'from now on you will be catching people'. In John's Gospel (4.10–15), Jesus offers a Samaritan woman 'living water'. In his first letter to the Corinthian church (3.10–15), Paul talks about building on the foundation that is Jesus Christ. There are many ways of interpreting such images according to the vocation and calling of individual Christians. The challenge for each of us is to discover the specific way in which we can be true both to our common vocation in Christ, and also our particular and personal vocation. This is not just about finding a job, or doing particular things; it is about participation in the transformation of life that is our Christian vocation.

Fraser Watts[2] rightly cautions against seeing any simple correspondence between the teachings of Jesus in the Gospels and contemporary psychology. However, our self-understanding is now so psychologically informed that we cannot completely avoid exploring how the transformation of life that Christian discipleship entails might be worked out in practice. Watts suggests that Jungian analytical psychology offers a helpful analogy. The Self archetype (to be distinguished from the ego as 'self'), according to Jung, represents the goal of human wholeness, our best possible destiny, as it were. However, it is more than just a goal. The Self is the image of God within the human psyche. As Watts suggests, 'The Self "calls" the ego towards it, rather as Jesus calls his disciples to him.'[3]

Experiences of voices calling people to particular Christian vocations might well be understood within this vein. They may well come from within, but this does not preclude the possibility that (at least sometimes) they are divinely inspired. In my research I was privileged to hear many accounts of this kind. The study sample was not systematically ascertained, and the research was not designed to provide quantitative data, but voices that might be understood as

2 Watts (2007).

3 Watts (2007, p.68).

calling someone to a particular vocation were amongst the commonest that were related to me.

The first example of this kind I present here is that of Wendy. Wendy's voice spoke only a single word. It was the context of this experience that proved to be vocationally significant.

WENDY'S STORY

My experience of hearing what I believe was God saying my name 'Wendy' occurred some 20 years ago. At that time I regularly attended a mid-week Holy Communion in a large 800-year-old village church where we sat in a semi-circle in the Lady Chapel area. One morning I sat down and joined the other 10 or so people already there in silent prayer prior to the service starting. As I sat there with eyes closed, I distinctly heard my name 'Wendy'. I opened my eyes to see who had said it, but everyone had their eyes closed, silently praying. I was convinced then, as I still am, that it was God's voice I heard. I cannot explain why I was and am so sure. It occurred around the time I was exploring a vocation, which developed some seven years later in me being licensed as a reader.

The experience of hearing one's name spoken out loud is not uncommon.[4] It does not usually seem to have spiritual or religious significance. The significance that it acquired here was because of the interpretation that Wendy placed on it in her particular context – at a service of Holy Communion, and at a point in her life when she was exploring a vocation. Of course, another person might have interpreted things differently, but it is still significant that the voice came at this particular turning point in her life, and in this particular place.

The next two stories provide examples of calling to a vocation in ordained ministry. In both cases, the voice is much more specific in relation to this particular calling, albeit also brief.

4 For example, in one study, 57 per cent of 375 students had had an experience of this kind (Posey and Losch 1983). Barrett and Etheridge (1992) reported similar findings (64 per cent) amongst students, and Millham and Easton (1998) reported a slightly lower figure (42 per cent) in a group of mental health nurses.

BEDE'S[5] STORY

The context was during evensong in Durham Cathedral, probably in August 1983. I was with my late father. While the Magnificat was being sung, there was a strong sense of leaving my body and going into a hot, yellowy and steamy place, totally unknown to me.

A firm voice then said, 'Be a priest.' Whoever spoke to me was near, but behind me. It is unclear now why I did not turn round to find out. I do not recall seeing anyone else there. I then remember returning to myself.

To say that I was frightened is, at best, an understatement. Though I lost track of time, I do not think this experience lasted long.

The experience was unanticipated, extremely sudden and powerful. I have never been able to forget [it] as it has been a significant factor in my life, together with its attendant consequences.

URSULA'S FIRST EXPERIENCE

I have had the experience of hearing a voice on two occasions in my life.[6] In writing about them I have added something of the context, which I hope is useful.

The first experience took place in 1979 when I was 45. In the background were many changes in my life and in church life. I had been a mature student and during my time at university had met professional women and been introduced to feminism. Within the church there were debates about the possibility of the ordination of women to the priesthood. I was also much involved in church life locally and in the diocese.

I was at the service of ordination in St Ninian's Cathedral, Perth, of a young man I knew. As he was kneeling before the bishop, I heard very clearly in my head a voice saying 'You should be there.' I did not share this with anyone, but felt that it was God calling me to be ordained. I had been involved in a very general way in the discussions about the ordination of women, but for me this meant it was about me! I was able to go on to be a deaconess, then deacon and to be among the first women to be ordained priest in 1994.

5 Pseudonym.

6 For an account of the second such experience, see Chapter 5.

A step such as following a call to ordained ministry is a once in a lifetime experience. However, it is only a first step towards a life of service to the Church. It is therefore necessarily followed by further steps, and more decisions to be made. Teresa of Calcutta spoke of the 'call within a call' that she received when she heard a voice pleading with her to serve the poor.[7] For most parish clergy, the questions will be more about 'where' than 'whom' to serve. Ravi Holy provides an account of the part that an inner voice played in guiding him to serve as vicar of the Wye group of churches in Kent.

RAVI'S STORY

In the same way that I had felt called into the ordained ministry 10 years before, when I first started praying about where God wanted me to go when my curacy ended, I very much felt him calling me out of the city and into the country. (My curacy was in Battersea; I am now in Wye, East Kent.)

Now I know that not everyone's comfortable with the language of 'God told me' this, that or the other, and often when I use a phrase like 'I felt God say' I'll stress that I don't mean an audible voice: God 'speaks' through events, circumstances or what might appear to be coincidences to the untrained eye. But on this occasion, it really was like hearing a voice...

I'd gone into my garden to pray late at night (which is not something I do that often, but I just felt the need to), and as soon as I said 'Lord, speak to me about my next post', the following words flashed through my mind: 'Go to where the sky is black and the Lord will be your light.'

Now, however villagey South Battersea may be, it's still in the middle of a huge metropolis so, even at midnight, the sky was a kind of orangey-grey colour, and that's what I was looking at as I heard or rather saw these words in my mind. So it seemed immediately obvious to me that God was saying don't be afraid to go to the country – where the sky is black because there's less light pollution – because all that counts is being where I want you to be, so go where the sky is black, and I will be your light.

---

7 Kolodiejchuk (2007, p.40). See also Cook (2018, pp.161–162).

Having accepted the job, my wife and I travelled down to start work on the vicarage and during that visit I met two key members of the congregation who invited me to be part of a project which was effectively the answer to something I'd been praying about for over 15 years – and which is now a significant part of my ministry. So, I would go so far as to say that if I'd gone to any other parish in the UK – or even the world – I wouldn't have discovered my destiny, my calling within my calling.

The final example in this section is unusual (at least amongst the stories that were provided to me in the course of this research) in that a voice provides guidance not about the vocation of the person hearing the voice, but rather about the vocation of another person. Liz, as a Diocesan Director of Ordinands (DDO), had particular responsibility for helping candidates exploring a vocation to ordained ministry. As she relates, the experience of hearing a voice was not completely unique for her, but it was certainly not a common occurrence.

LIZ'S STORY

In about 2001, when I was one of two Diocesan Directors of Ordinands (DDOs) for my diocese, I was present at the Diocesan Conference held at Butlin's at Bognor Regis. Between talks, I was stopped by someone I had not met before who asked to talk to me about ordination. We sat down to have a coffee together and she introduced herself as Ann. She told me that her husband had been to see my colleague, the 'other' DDO, and that he had said that he could not recognize that her husband had a vocation. Ann wanted to explain to me why she thought her husband did have a vocation, and to ask me if I would see him in place of my colleague. My primary thought was that I was going to find it difficult to get Ann to accept that as DDOs my colleague and I nearly always agreed with each other (as we worked by criteria and not personal likes and dislikes), and that it was my colleague she would need to persuade to refer her husband to me, if I saw him at all. I guessed she would see this as a sort of 'stitch up' and would feel quite angry about it. As she was speaking I heard a voice outside myself, not loud, and not with a recognizable accent or intonation, and I found myself just repeating what the voice had said. The words were: 'It's not your husband who should be ordained; it's you.'

Ann, who at the time was speaking in a quite impassioned way about why her husband should be allowed to go forward for ordination, went silent. She came from a tradition in the C of E [Church of England] that did not believe in women's ordination and was clearly taken aback. I suggested she think about it and got back to me in the future if she wished to.

In conclusion, Ann has been ordained for some years now. Her husband has remained, happily, as a layperson.

The voice and its message was as much a surprise to me as to Ann. To the best of my knowledge and awareness, I had not consciously had the thought before hearing the words. I was also not aware of a conscious decision that I would repeat the words. I was DDO in the diocese for 18 years, and over that time I heard what seemed to be the same voice a couple of other times when interviewing people, always suggesting something I was not aware of consciously thinking myself, always surprising me by the content. In each case the voice's words proved 'true' for the hearer. I have also, on very rare occasions, heard the same voice when at prayer. Again, the voice has always said something that has surprised me and been outside my conscious thinking.

Liz's observation that the voice was always surprising, that it said things that she was not conscious of, echoes with various other accounts provided in this book. Voices are experienced as 'not the kind of thing I would have thought'. Liz is careful in her description of the phenomenology, and does not go beyond the bare facts. Although Liz does not say this, it would be easy to conclude that this voice came from God, but in some ways that interpretation might obscure rather than clarify what happened. Her account is the more powerful for its simplicity and objectivity. The reader can place his or her own interpretation on the facts, but the facts speak powerfully for themselves. The voice that Liz heard changed the course of Ann's life.

Calling voices

Calling and vocation are important issues for everyone, but for those who believe in God they are perhaps especially so, or at least they are especially complicated. It is hard enough for any young person to know themself well enough to make the crucial decisions that commit them to a particular job, partner or way of life. (Perhaps this is why several of the examples given in this chapter concern a change of course in later life.) Such decisions become especially complicated when it is not just 'my' decision, but a question of hearing what God is calling me to. The theological construction of vocation as what God calls someone to, as opposed to simply what they themselves choose to do, might seem especially psychologically receptive to the possibility of hearing a voice. As Tanya Luhrmann's research shows,[8] expectancy of such experiences within some Christian traditions may play a part in fostering them. There are also few other decisions in life that are as absorbing of our attention, time and emotions. Given that attention and absorption seem to be important psychological factors in generating such experiences, it is perhaps more surprising that they do not occur in this context even more commonly than they appear to do.

8 Luhrmann (2012); see also Cook (2018, pp.169–170, 183–185).

Chapter 4

Crisis

Some voices are heard in extremis. Whilst I am unable to quantify the frequency with which such voices are heard (either amongst Christians or in the wider population), such voices do appear to be qualitatively different than those which are heard more regularly and frequently during daily life or in prayer (such as, for example, those reported in other chapters of this book by Errol, Lucy, Klair or Kit).

The taxonomy of voices that I have adopted is imperfect insofar as its categories are not mutually exclusive. The story of Sundar Singh, for example, provides a good example of an experience of conversion occurring at a time of crisis. Brought up in colonial India, in a Sikh family, as a young person Sundar took an interest in a variety of religions, yet despised Christianity. Finding no peace, he was on the verge of suicide when he had a vision of Christ, who said to him (in Hindustani), 'How long will you persecute me? I have come to save you; you were praying to know the right way. Why do you not take it?'[1] Finding, at last, the peace that he had been searching for, Sundar became a Christian missionary, albeit a controversial figure who did not adopt any of the conventional religious roles available to him.[2]

Some of the narratives in other chapters of this book are also associated with times of crisis, and I am not suggesting that my categories do not overlap. However, I have selected here some stories

1 Quoted in Streeter and Appasamy (1926).

2 For further discussion, see Cook (2018, pp.135–136).

that are associated with particularly significant crises, concerned with matters of life and death.

None of my respondents reported 'near-death experiences', but voices are sometimes documented amongst the constellation of phenomena that such experiences comprise.[3] The first three stories are all concerned with sudden and unexpected circumstances, as a result of which the person hearing the voice might have died. For Harold and Margaret, both of whom got into difficulties whilst swimming in the sea, it was only their own lives that were at risk. Their voices told them what to do in the emergency. Margaret is convinced that the voice saved her life. The third story provides accounts of two incidents experienced by the same person, both in the context of driving alone on a long journey. The first of these, whilst driving on a motorway, might easily have ended with multiple deaths. In this context, the voice offers reassurance amidst the crisis. In the second incident, where the presence of an embodied human speaker cannot be excluded, the voice offers instructions about what to do.

HAROLD'S[4] STORY

I was attending a Crusader camp, under canvas, in the summer of 1948 at Polzeath in Cornwall, taking the opportunity most afternoons to go for a swim in the sea. I was 14 years old.

Late one afternoon whilst swimming I was caught in a 'rip tide'. Fortunately, being a reasonably good swimmer, it did not concern me too much at first, but very soon I found that the harder I swam, the further the shoreline receded into the distance. Concern set in.

Shortly afterwards I heard a voice. I cannot describe it now with total accuracy, but the voice was telling me, 'Stay calm, relax, float on your back, go with the strong current and when it eases swim back to the shore. All will be well.'

And so it was. I floated on my back and when, about three hundred yards from the shoreline, the water became more calm, and I swam back to the beach. No one had missed me!!

3 Cook (2018, pp.163–164).

4 Pseudonym.

MARGARET'S STORY

After the war we used to go on holiday to stay with my grandfather. It was a marvellous place for children; the house was less than a hundred yards from the shore, which consisted of a wide stretch of tumbled rocks and pools, bordered by a rim of high rocks for some distance along the water's edge. We would make our camp on one of these which was lower than the others, and had at its base a flat stretch, five or six feet wide, bordering the deep water; from here we would launch ourselves to swim.

I never went back there till after my father's death, when my mother and I decided to visit the family; she was in her mid-seventies at this time, and I was in my early fifties. It must, I think, have been August; the weather on the day in question was cloudy, but not particularly cold. I suggested visiting our old haunts, and when we got there I said I had to have a quick dip for old times' sake. My mother stayed in the car; I took my bathing things, went down the slope to the rocks below and crossed to our accustomed place. When I jumped in I was taken by surprise at how cold it was – I gasped at the shock, and started to swim, but almost immediately found I was seizing up. After no more than two or three strokes I decided not to stay in any longer, and turned towards the rocks – only to realize that I could not remember how to get out. The ledge of flat rock was a good eighteen inches above the surface of the water; even as a fit youngster I could not have hauled myself out with my hands to that height.

No matter how I racked my brains I could not recall what we did to get back onto the flat rock. Meanwhile my movements were getting slower all the time; I seemed to be closing down (I now know that I had what is called cold water shock, which is often fatal). I realized I was in danger; I thought, quite unemotionally, 'If I don't get out of this quickly I am going to die – but I don't know how to get out. I've got to swim past the high rocks – but I don't think I'll be able to swim that far.' At that point I said (not aloud), 'Please God help me: I don't know how to get out' – and a voice said, clearly and quite loudly, 'There is a step under the water.' It was not in my head, or at least I didn't experience it as such: it was about six feet away, on the left. I can't describe it as having any characteristics: it wasn't a male voice, or a female voice, just very anonymously but definitely a voice. Immediately I turned back towards the flat rock again, which I had turned away from, and started to swim towards one end of it – not of my own volition, as it seemed, but as if something was pulling me through the water in that direction, as an angler pulls a fish. As I came up to the wall of rock I pulled my legs up under me and 'stepped' out questioningly in front of me. My foot landed on flat rock.

Some days later I regained a dim recollection of having used that step when getting into the sea when the tide was very low. I never remembered using it for getting out again, though obviously we must have done. Without the voice I would have died in the water; I have little doubt of that. But I prayed, and salvation came.

CARIS'S[5] STORY

Episodes that seem to be out of time, in some way supernatural, which have nothing to do with logic and reason, remain in the memory long afterwards and can be recalled almost as clearly as when they occurred. But, to seek to ensure my recollection, I wrote a poem shortly after the first incident, described below.

In 2006, on a gloriously sunny May morning at around 6.30am, I was on the M5 motorway, driving north from Stroud, in the middle lane. The traffic was very heavy, streams of cars in all three lanes. Suddenly, in the flat land near Tewkesbury, a deer climbed up on the bank overlooking the motorway. It wobbled and in that moment the driver in the outside lane reckoned that, if the deer jumped, it would land in front of my car and so he swerved wildly, anticipating the avoiding action that I might take. At that moment, a clear male voice spoke from the rear of my car: 'It's all right, I'm here...' Strength poured down both arms, one of which I had recently broken, and I held the steering wheel firmly. The deer did jump and I killed the deer outright; there was no car crash and all humans were safe. Was my 'passenger' Jesus; was he an angel? I do not know, but am sure that I received a supernatural visitor.

Another year, when trying to find the hotel into which I had been booked, I realized that I was hopelessly lost. It was at the end of a busy day, perhaps 6.30pm. I turned off the main road – there was no signpost

5 Pseudonym.

that I recall – and found myself on a small road going through woodland. It wasn't dark – but the light was dappled. Then I saw a large lorry parked on the left-hand verge. I stopped and got out of the car – a stupid thing for a lone woman driver to do at a lonely place in the evening. A youngish middle-aged man, who neither looked nor sounded like a lorry driver, suddenly appeared around the side of the lorry and said 'You shouldn't be here.' 'I know', I replied 'but I'm lost. I need to get to (such and such) hotel.' Speaking clearly, he gave me perfect instructions as to how to get there, turned round and seemed to vanish. He sounded just like my M5 rescuer. The directions were impeccably accurate (I am not good at remembering detail), and I drove confidently to the hotel, arriving perfectly at ease. Again I could not say who my rescuer was, but felt sure that this very real sounding and seeming person was different.

I feel immensely blessed to have received these gifts. I wrote a poem about the first incident and, as a consequence, can recall it far more clearly than the woodland encounter.

AN ACT OF GRACE

Early summer morning; glancing light; slight mist;
Trees taking shape with the dawn;
A sense of expectation of the new day ahead.
Motorway curiously busy; streaming cars in all three lanes. Fast.
A lone driver in the middle lane singing.
The deer – who knows what its instinct was – no sense at all
of its imminent danger appeared on the bank. Stood uncertainly.
And leapt.
Time stood still for the middle lane driver. The only way
out of a multiple crash was to hold hard and kill this sleek beauty.
Anticipating avoiding action, the driver on the outside swerved
and this gentle voice said to the driver in the middle 'It's all right, I'm here.'
Waves of energy flowed through both arms as she held the wheel hard.
And didn't veer to either side.
Dreadful impact killed the deer.
And humans went their way.
Grace and peace flowed through the driver in the middle lane.
Thanks be to God.

The next story, which takes place at the beginning rather than the end of a life, was previously published in Sue Talbot's *The Confessions of a Reluctant Mystic*, which is now out of print. As one of the respondents who participated in my research, Sue kindly agreed to the story being reproduced here. In a letter to her son, written after he was born, Sue describes the final stages of his birth:

SUE'S STORY

The body that was mine was going through what appeared to be something akin to convulsions but now there was no pain and within a world of quietness I hear a still, small voice speak.

One day, my son, I will read you the story of Elijah who also heard a still, small voice... I wonder if the voice is the same. What did it sound like?... It was so clear, so like hearing a human voice, so very, very like, but it was a hearing that was somehow on the inside. Without the help of my ears, words were suddenly there in my mind that I had not gone through the bother of actually thinking...it was...it was a warning, a preparation, a strange encouragement.

> As this is, so your dying will be...

That was all...so little and yet so much.

For in that hearing was also a knowing: that all this was for Life; that there were two realities, the inner and the outer; that what things looked like on the outside was not necessarily what was going on on the inside; that both realities were true. There was the body in extremity but the inner self was in a world of quiet, waiting; waiting for the life to be born. That time I was waiting for you, the next time it would be my life that would be waiting to be born, to be pushed by the processes of dying into life. I would be awaiting and struggling to my own beginning.[6]

The final two stories included in this chapter return to the theme of death. In both cases, the crisis is the death of another person. Jean was a child at the time of the death of her grandmother, and identified

6 Talbot (1986, pp.175–176).

the voice that she heard as that of an angel. Relatively little has been written about spiritual or religious aspects of voice hearing in children,[7] and this is somewhat surprising, as somewhere between 5 and 32 per cent of children and adolescents have heard voices.[8] There is tentative evidence that children who have imaginary companions may be more likely to hear voices.[9]

Whereas Jean heard only two words, which enabled adult help to be summoned, Naomi had more of a dialogue with God (see Chapter 4, this book). Jean's voice drew attention to a death that had already taken place. Naomi's voice anticipated a death, and thus enabled her to have a final, and much valued, conversation with the person concerned.

JEAN'S STORY

I was 11 or 12 years of age at the time. I was asleep in bed and was woken by a clear voice in my head which said, 'Call Daddy.' This, surely, could only be my grandmother who was sleeping in the room below mine. I dutifully went into my parents' room and my father went to see my grandmother. The voice, as I stressed to my parents the next day, could not have been my grandmother's as she was a frail 89 years of age and this voice was young and clear, and lovely in quality. I went back to sleep and woke in the morning to a quiet house, having heard nothing else throughout the night. The normal routine followed except that I and my brother were told that grandma had died in the night. I was amazed by the strange and wonderful atmosphere in the house and became famous for saying, over breakfast, 'Isn't it nice when someone dies?'

I had always told myself that an angel had spoken to me as I thought then that angels were female.

7 An interesting account is provided by Coles (1990, pp.69–97), who offers a case study of four children – one Muslim, one Jewish, and two Christian – who report having heard the voice of God.

8 McCarthy-Jones (2012, pp.177–178).

9 McCarthy-Jones (2012, p.257).

NAOMI'S STORY: HEARING GOD'S VOICE

It was July 1981. The previous September, as an evangelical Christian, I had made a commitment. Aged 40+, I was working as a primary school teacher. One of my neighbours, Alan, who was in his seventies, had lost his wife some time previously. I started visiting him and taking him for drives, inviting him for meals, etc., and we became very close friends. Then, one Saturday, I heard from our curate that Alan had had a heart attack while visiting his sister, and had been taken into intensive care in Worcester, 25 miles away. The curate was able to visit, as were his close relatives, but not me. I was not a relative. All I could do was to pray.

The following Wednesday, about 4.30pm, I was in my classroom preparing lessons for the next day. I had just put a pile of children's needlework in a cupboard when I heard a voice. I was alone in the room and I knew that had there been anyone else present they would not have heard it. But to me it was a real voice, and I recognized it as the voice of God. The voice said, 'Go home and ring up Ronkswood Hospital.' I replied 'But Lord, I can't do that. I have the children's maths to get ready for tomorrow.' The voice replied, 'That's all right. Get the children's work ready and then go home and ring up the hospital.' (I should add that my classroom was in a separate building so I didn't have access to the school telephone.) Then, panic! 'Lord, I can't find my maths record book.' 'Look under that pile of needlework you've just put away.' I looked; there was the record book. I got the following day's work ready, went home and rang the hospital. They told me that Alan had just been moved to a medical ward and yes, I could come and visit him. After a quick meal I drove to Worcester. Alan was sitting up in bed, very bright and seemingly much better. I spent a precious hour with him, and then drove home promising to come again to visit. But that was not to be. In the middle of the night Alan had another, fatal, heart attack. We would not see each other again in this life.

The only explanation I have for this testimony is that on his move to the medical ward Alan had prayed and asked God to make it possible for me to see him for what would be the last time. That visit remains one of my most precious memories.

Voices in crisis

There is some evidence to suggest that hallucinations might be more likely to occur in states of high arousal and in environments with high sensory input.[10] High arousal states, such as those experienced by Harold, Margaret or Caris in their respective crises, might therefore be ones in which the hearing of a voice would be more likely. However, this does not explain either the content or the interpretation of the voices heard. Margaret, Caris, Jean and Naomi were given instructions by their voices. Caris and Sue were offered comfort, encouragement or reassurance.

None of the voices described here need necessarily be understood as coming from a religious or spiritual source, but all of them were interpreted in this way by those who heard them. Harold was attending a Christian camp at the time, and the spiritual significance of the event is left largely implicit. Margaret prayed in the midst of her crisis and believed the voice was an answer to her prayer. Caris speculates that her mystery 'passenger' might have been Jesus or an angel, but it was not just a voice, and she later made a clear link with the voice that she heard (even though this may only have been a human voice) in the midst of another crisis. Sue does not tell us unambiguously whose voice she heard, but it was only 'like' a human voice, and the reflections on reality and on life and death that it evoked have a semi-mystical quality. Jean, a child at the time, identified her voice as angelic. Naomi interpreted her voice as God's answer to the prayers of her neighbour.

At least two or three of these voices, and perhaps more, apparently 'knew' things that the person hearing them did not know. Margaret speculates that this might have come from something dimly remembered. For Jean and Naomi, the knowing was more a matter of timing. Their voices were heard at precisely the right moment to enable action to be taken at the time of (or before) a death.

Spirituality and religion seek to provide meaning and comfort in the context of life and death. Each of the voices reported in this chapter

10 There may also be an association with the opposite – that is, low arousal and quiet or unstimulating surroundings. See Cook (2018, pp.182–183); McCarthy-Jones (2012, pp.261, 266); and Slade and Bentall (1988, pp.89–92, 143–145).

assisted to this end, either directly (by way of comfort and reassurance) or indirectly, by way of the interpretation of the experience that the hearer of the voice came to adopt. Do these voices also represent divine intervention at moments of crisis? Answers to this question will clearly depend on the faith of the reader, but I do not think that this can be ruled out. There is no clear reason, theologically or scientifically, why we might not understand some voices as being revelatory, or as in some other way representing divine intervention.[11] We return to this question in the final two chapters of the book.

11 Cook (2018, pp.189–228).

Chapter 5

Comfort

Judeo-Christian scripture has numerous references to God comforting his people. Perhaps the most famous of all such passages is to be found in Psalm 23.1–4:

> The LORD is my shepherd, I shall not want. He makes me lie down in green pastures; he leads me beside still waters; he restores my soul. He leads me in right paths for his name's sake. Even though I walk through the darkest valley, I fear no evil; for you are with me; your rod and your staff – they comfort me.

Isaiah refers to God comforting his people as a mother comforts her children (66.13). In the Sermon on the Mount, Jesus refers to those who mourn as blessed, 'for they will be comforted' (Matthew 5.4).

In his second letter to the Thessalonians, it is Paul's prayer that God will comfort his people:

> Now may our Lord Jesus Christ himself and God our Father, who loved us and through grace gave us eternal comfort and good hope, comfort your hearts and strengthen them in every good work and word. (2.16–17)

It is, of course, easy to select such verses and ignore passages of judgement. There are indeed passages of scripture that might be very discomforting, but this does not negate God's comfort for those who are distressed. Some of the voices that my respondents reported to me echoed this theme, and this chapter is devoted to them. The emphasis here is thus on the way in which some voices, particularly the voice of God, provide emotional reassurance, consolation or affirmation amidst difficult circumstances.

The first such story I present here is as much about healing of past trauma as it is about comfort for present distress, and I do not pretend that these can be separated. However, Judith speaks of the 'immense compassion' that was conveyed by Jesus in the words that she heard, and it is clear that the hearing of his voice was a very reassuring and comforting experience for her.

JUDITH'S STORY

My experience of 'hearing' Jesus speaking to me came about like this. It was in August 1992 and I was on an individually guided retreat at Burford Abbey. I had been helped by the monk who was guiding me to return to a painful time in my childhood. By his patient attention I was enabled to speak about the forsaken, abandoned child who was me, but who I had buried and spent years unable to acknowledge and bring to God. After our session I prayed before the Blessed Sacrament in the chapel and cried for that lost, vulnerable child, and all the abandoned, especially our dear Lord himself, who had cried out, 'My God, my God, why have you forsaken me?' While I'd been speaking to my guide, it had been the lost nine-year-old crying. And then it was the 'me' present in the chapel crying for her, and then I took her by the hand to Jesus, and it was me myself crying, and he said, 'I've been waiting a long time for you to bring me this.' The words Jesus spoke to me were spoken with immense compassion.

I knew it was Jesus who spoke those words to me, although it wasn't an auditory voice. It was a profound experience which I've never forgotten, and I wrote about it straightaway in my journal, which I've just quoted from here.

The next two accounts relate to experiences of death. The first, related by Ursula (whose experience of calling to ministry is related in Chapter 3), concerns the grief that she experienced following the death of her husband. The second, related by Lucy (a Korean doctor whose story is told at greater length in Chapter 7), concerns the death of one of her patients.

URSULA'S SECOND EXPERIENCE[1]

I retired from full-time ministry in 1999 and got married to Peter whom I had met not long before. He had had much tragedy in his life and was generally angry with the God in whom he did not believe! He was puzzled about my faith, but was respectful. Although we did have some intense discussions, neither of us changed our views. He died in 2011, from cancer. Before he died he had left definite instructions about what was to be done and that there was not to be a service in church. I prepared the liturgy, trying to be both respectful of his views yet wanting to commend him to the God I believed in. After the funeral, in my grief, I became very troubled by some views that some Christians express that only Christians go to heaven! I cannot believe that God condemns any to hell, even if there is hell, but for a time I struggled theologically.

It was about four months after Peter's death and I was sitting quietly at the kitchen table. I became aware of a presence behind me; it felt good. Then I heard a voice say twice 'Peter is alright' and I sensed what I can only describe as an angelic presence. It was both a reassuring and a comforting experience, and from that time I no longer had the troubling thoughts about life after death. Why angels? I had earlier been listening to 'The Dream of Gerontius', so maybe that gave me the words to express the experience. Even six years on, that moment means much to me. Remembering reminds me of the love that we had for each other.

LUCY: ALICE[2] IS WITH ANGELS

In 2018, I came back to South Korea and started to work in a small Buddhist hospice. One of my patients there, whom I will refer to as 'Alice', was a 79-year-old woman who had suffered from severe shortness of breath (due to chronic obstructive pulmonary disease and congestive heart failure) for a long time. Large university hospitals tagged her as 'hopeless', and her family moved her to this hospice for supportive and palliative care.

1 For an account of the first experience, see Chapter 3.
2 Lucy and Alice are pseudonyms.

One day, Alice had a serious myocardial infarction. I started medical therapy for palliation (including morphine for relieving the pain and serious breathlessness). For several days before her death, her family and I watched her extreme suffering with serious breathlessness.

It was a great privilege to take care of Alice during her last days. I thanked God for letting me have this role. It was an honour.

One night, after prescribing more morphine for her, I sat down in front of my statue of Mary for my routine night prayers. Immediately after I sat down and started to pray, I was aware of strong energy from the statue flowing to my heart accompanied by overwhelming voices. It was a very unusual experience. On most occasions, voices that I hear are very subtle, like a breeze, so I must concentrate carefully to catch them and discern what they are saying. On this occasion, the voice flowing to my heart was overwhelming, and the message was so clear that I could not miss it: 'Do not worry. Alice is with angels.' Then I had a mental image of golden lights surrounding Alice's bed.

At the time, I could not understand what it all meant, but immediately after I finished my prayer, I received a call informing me of Alice's death. It is hard to express how I felt. I was surprised, stunned, thankful and relieved. I felt that I was under the protection and guidance of Mary. This was what Mary wanted to tell me! I shared my spiritual experience with the bereaved family. Although they were all sincere Buddhists, it became a great consolation for them and for me too.

The next account, which has a mystical quality, although it relates to a context of a chronic illness, on later reflection seemed to have much wider significance and to be given as much for others as for Stephen himself. Stephen has contributed two experiences to the present book. This account is of his second experience. The first experience is related in Chapter 6, and there he also has some interesting reflections to offer on how he understands both experiences.

STEPHEN'S FIRST EXPERIENCE

A more profound experience occurred about five years ago in the chapel of an Anglican theological college where my wife was training for the priesthood. We both attended an evening service of Benediction, something I'd always experienced as a sacred time, but which my wife had never taken part in.

On that particular day I was feeling rather ill. My life had been significantly limited by ME/CFS[3] for about 14 years by then. However, I decided to go anyway and looked forward to the quiet atmosphere and sense of mystery. During the silent adoration part of the service it suddenly seemed as if the monstrance (the cross that holds the consecrated host) was both on the altar and within me, somehow in two places at once. There was a sense of unity and a feeling of joy, of being lovingly welcomed and honoured in a place where God was more fully present. The parable of the great feast in Luke 14.15–23, where the abject and crippled are invited to share the banquet, seemed a good description of how I felt. It was at that point I 'heard' in my head a distinctly male voice say 'You are blessed beyond measure.' I felt very humbled and overwhelmed at this point, feeling that this was a gift that of course I didn't merit but that came from God's grace. Afterwards I told my wife about it and cried due to the overwhelming nature of the experience. In processing the occurrence afterwards, it seemed that I'd been given a taste of what awaits all who seek a relationship with God, both as an encouragement to me during a difficult period of illness, and to others should it ever be appropriate to speak of it.

The final account to be included in this chapter is also the longest in this section of the book. Whilst the voice itself remains something of a mystery, the context in which it was heard is very significant. It is also a story of healing. Whilst I have referred to contributors throughout this book by first name only, I have this contributor's permission to disclose that she is the wife of Harold Koenig, who has published widely on spirituality and health, and is the leading clinical researcher in this field worldwide. When I have shared a conference platform with Charmin and Harold, delegates have spoken to me afterwards of the powerful effect on them of the combination of Charmin's personal and emotional testimony and Harold's cutting-edge research and academic rigour.

---

3 Myalgic encephalomyelitis, or chronic fatigue syndrome.

CHARMIN'S STORY: TO DEPRESSION AND BACK

> You may be depressed, angry, bitter and hurting…but I'm here to tell you that God cares.

I would like to share with you something I was allowed to experience lately. It is very difficult trying to relate all the feelings and emotions involved in such an experience, but if even one heart is spoken to through this story, it will have served its purpose.

June 1986 proved to be a very hectic month for me. Moving from Missouri to my folk's home in Iowa for a short two-week stay before moving everything to North Carolina was only the beginning. I had to finish the final plans for my wedding and keep up with all the pre-wedding happenings. After the wedding and returning from our honeymoon, we immediately left in our loaded-down truck for North Carolina. It wasn't long before we were settled in our beautiful home and both busy with our new jobs. After just a few short weeks, we found the church that we wanted to get involved with. All in all, everything was going fairly smoothly.

After about three months of marriage, I noticed some change within me, a type of mood swing. I have always been a pretty 'up' person, so what I was feeling was confusing to me. It was subtle at first, but as time wore on, it took less and less to bring me down, to make me cry. I began to have trouble sleeping and I lost my appetite. I tried to sort out my feelings and talk them over with my husband, yet I just couldn't put my finger on what was going on. So, instead of communicating, I would just withdraw from him.

I felt so many things – frustration, anger, resentment and bitterness. The more I thought about how I was feeling inside and acting towards my husband, the angrier I became at myself. What was happening? I was a Christian – how could I be feeling like this? Nothing was making sense. I just didn't understand. I prayed and prayed, yet feeling worse, I had little faith that God was even hearing me. My husband is a physician and I am a nurse, so we both recognized the signs of depression, yet I couldn't admit it to myself let alone to him. If I was depressed, I was a failure as a Christian, wasn't I?

Mid-November, I hit rock bottom. I could hardly force myself to smile. I hurt so badly inside and prayed earnestly that God would take the pain away by letting me die. I knew the strain on my husband was beginning to take its toll also, so I knew he would be better off without me. I had cried out several times for help and my pastor was always available to me with gentle, yet firm counsel. He, too, felt we were dealing with some sort of depression. He shared with me some scripture where even David struggled with the same feelings I was having. 'Be gracious to me, O Lord, for my bones are dismayed, and my soul is greatly dismayed. But thou, O Lord, how long? I am weary with my sighing, every night I make my bed swim, I dissolve my couch with my tears.' It was hard to believe anyone could hurt as deeply as I was right then, and yet here was David crying out to the Lord the same question I had been asking. 'How long will I be like this?' Just as the Lord heard David's cries, he also heard mine.

On Friday, December 12th, I ended up having to leave work early. My mind wasn't capable of taking care of myself, let alone my patients. I felt emotionally and physically drained and yet was unable to rest. We had recently gotten our Christmas tree and as yet I had not been in any mood to decorate it. It took everything within me to try it now, but I just felt like I had to make an effort. Pastor Dave had encouraged me to listen to praise and worship tapes as much as possible, so I started to play a new one and just stared into the blinking lights. 'Lord', I said, 'Here it is, my first Christmas with my husband but I'm dreading it. I'm dreading the holidays and I'm dreading tomorrow. Please God. Please help me.'

Some words interjected with the praise music caught my attention. I heard a man speak these words: 'You may be depressed, angry, bitter and hurting. You may feel like you don't even want to go on, but I'm here to tell you that God cares. He is well aware of your situation and it is all in His timing. Sometimes He must allow us to hurt deeply in order for us to be used greatly.'

Tears flooded from my eyes as I simply said, 'Thank you Jesus.' With those words, as the tears freely flowed, joy filled my entire being, a joy I hadn't felt in months. The joy of the Lord, what strength it offers. I couldn't wait for my husband to get home, something I had previously dreaded. When he came in and asked me about my day, I could only smile and say, 'Honey, I'm almost normal again. It's going to be okay now.' We fell into each other's arms thanking God for His faithfulness and mercy.

I explained to him about how the tape had really ministered to my heart and was anxious to play it for him before we had to leave for the evening. I quickly ran it through, fast forwarding it at times, but could not find the words. The next day I played both sides of the tape twice and the words never appeared. God had chosen that tape as a vehicle to speak to my heart. It was so amazing and yet to me the real miracle wasn't so much those words appearing on the tape, but the healing power of God. He brought me out of the very depths of darkness and despair and sat me instantly back on solid rock, filling my life with meaning once again.

Comforting voices

I commented at the end of the last chapter that spirituality and religion seek to provide meaning and comfort in the context of life and death. Voices heard in crisis, as reported in that chapter, also have a comforting dimension to them. The voices reported in this present chapter similarly provided comfort, although with more of an emphasis on the emotional reassurance they provided some time after events rather than in the midst of them. Judith's voice related to childhood events many years previously. It was only four months after her husband's death that Ursula heard the voice that brought her comfort. In both of these stories, however, the timing was arguably crucial. Words of comfort spoken prematurely do not necessarily help.

Lucy's story is different in that she has had many experiences of hearing voices (as related in Chapter 7), and has learned when and how to listen, and how to interpret the voices. This story raises significant questions around professional practice, which I return to in Chapter 14, but Alice's family clearly found consolation in what Lucy heard, as did Lucy herself. Similarly, Stephen believed that the voice he heard was not for him alone, but was to be for the comfort of others.

Charmin's story brings together many, if not all, of these dimensions of comfort. The voice that she heard brought comfort and healing amidst an experience of depression and a period of difficult adjustment to married life. The story, as she has related it from public platforms, has also brought much comfort to others around the world.

Chapter 6

Confirming and Clarifying

Amidst uncertain or difficult circumstances, some voices seem to offer something more than just emotional comfort, but rather less than detailed guidance about exactly what to do next. I have thus devoted this chapter to voices that provide confirmation or clarification in the context of uncertainty. A particular course of action is confirmed, or clarification is gained about whether or not something is the right thing to do. Perhaps these voices may be characterized as concerned primarily with the resolution of doubt. Will things be okay, or won't they? Should I take this course of action, or not?

I am aware that there is overlap here with other chapters. In particular, some of the stories included here might equally have been well placed in Chapters 3, 4 or 5. They include at least some of the elements found in the stories included in Chapters 7 and 9. The decision to group them together in a chapter of their own should not be taken as a rigid categorization that implies lack of overlap with other kinds of voices. However, I think that it does draw attention to the way in which voices sometimes seem to intervene in the context of doubt, fear and uncertainty to confirm or clarify what should be done and to provide reassurance about what will happen.

The first two stories are very short and both occur in an emotionally difficult context. In Avril's story, the confirmation of calling is largely implicit, as the voice speaks only her name. In John's story, the voice provides reassurance that things will turn out well despite anxiety about the future for his children.

AVRIL'S STORY

I was at St Stephen's House, Oxford, in training for ordination. And the vice-principal had been giving us a talk about priesthood – one that made me feel utterly unworthy to be attempting to take this on. I was lying in bed that night full of anxiety about whether I was doing the right thing, whether the church had got it wrong, etc., etc., when I simply heard my name. I wasn't asking God for a response, I wasn't overtly praying (though probably I should have been); it was sudden and shocking. Both inside my head and out loud at the same time is the only way I can describe it.

JOHN'S STORY

On 4th April 1980 (Good Friday) my wife gave birth to triplets 12 weeks premature. They weighed 2lb 5oz, 2lb 6oz and 2lb 7oz. They were in intensive care. I can remember driving home from Kettering to Corby where we lived at the time and I heard a distinct voice behind me saying: 'Those little babies are going to be all right.' That proved to be the case. It's the only time I have had such an experience but still vividly remember it and could (until the road was upgraded) point to the exact spot.

In the next story, Stephen experiences doubt amidst his prayers. Should he devote his time to praying for others, or should he be devoting his attention to God? The voice confirms that he doesn't have to feel guilty, and gives him permission to do what he had previously resolved to do. As a psychotherapist, Stephen has some interesting reflections on how he comes to interpret his experience. He concludes that theological and psychological explanations are not incompatible.

STEPHEN'S SECOND EXPERIENCE

I have been given several mystical or 'peak' experiences, to use Abraham Maslow's phrase.[1] The first of these occurred when I was 16 years old. However, there have only been two in which I felt I was 'spoken to'. By this I mean it seemed as if the words came from someone or something other than my conscious ego. The first happened about nine or ten years ago during a time of meditation/silent prayer. I was simply trying to be still and sit consciously in God's presence. I had a feeling that I should be saying my daily intercessory prayers for others, rather than giving myself this time just to 'be' in God. At this point, however, an authoritative voice inside said: 'No, you don't have to', and I felt I was being given permission just to carry on with focusing on God. Accompanying this was the realization that other people's wellbeing was not dependent on my prayers. This communication was experienced as 'a still small voice' within – a strong thought, but one which seemed to come from outside my own conscious awareness.

Having trained as a psychotherapist some years ago, I am used to interpreting our inner life through the lenses of various analytic schools. Without taking away from the spiritual significance of the above experiences, it is possible to understand them from within a Jungian framework.

C.G. Jung considered that, as well as our personal ego, we each had an archetypal Self which resided on a deeper unconscious level. The Self both represents the totality of our psyche and acts as a guide/balancing force in enabling us to become fully integrated as an individual.[2] Jung also saw the Self as an image of God within. One could therefore posit that, in my case, the voices were communications from the unconscious Self attempting to re-balance unhelpful conscious attitudes. Jung himself speaks in several places of hearing voices during periods of psychological upheaval and growth.[3]

I am aware that it might be argued by some that such voice hearing is always the result of some psychological illness/imbalance. I cannot

1 Maslow (1964).

2 Jung (1983, p.224).

3 Jung (1983, p.199).

make sense of my own experiences using this view, since the fruit of the experiences was a greater and lasting degree of psychological wellbeing. On the other hand, if these experiences are in some way unusual, I'm quite prepared to accept that I may have some atypical neurology. Yet I see no reason why this cannot be used by God to bring about greater wholeness, or develop one's understanding of and relationship with the Divine.

The next story also provides an account of a voice that gives permission. The immediate context is one concerned with uncertainty about how to handle human relationships, but more significantly the voice leads Ellen into a new relationship with God. Two further, more recent, examples of Ellen's experiences are provided in Chapter 8.

ELLEN'S STORY: VOICE IN THE CATHEDRAL

I was visiting Barcelona on a business trip. I had never been to the Sagrada Familia before, in spite of several trips to Barcelona, and was keen to see it. I booked a flight to come into Barcelona a day early to do so. But I bumped into a high-level manager at my firm at the airport, who asked me to lunch...we had a good lunch and so when I returned to my room and sat down on the bed for a minute, I fell asleep. I didn't wake up until very late and so decided to get up early the following morning to go and see the cathedral.

When I arrived, I bought an audio tour and started looking around. After about a half-hour, I began to feel a bit odd, though, and then I heard a voice – it was not in my head, but outside of me. I was not hearing it with my ears – it was as though there was some other way I could hear besides my ears. If I had to ascribe a sex to it, I would say it was male. It told me that I should divorce my husband (I had been debating this for some time, and it was a source of real inner conflict for me) and that another person in my life was 'my gift to you'. In point of fact this other person had (and would do) several things that had a very positive impact on my life.

My initial reaction was one of shock and disbelief – more at the fact of hearing the voice than about what it was saying. I grew upset and the voice just kept repeating the same message over and over, as though to assure me that it was 'real', that I was not bonkers, and that it meant well. Eventually I understood and accepted it, and then it faded away. I was left sitting on a bench on the side of the cathedral. I cried quite a lot – shock, amazement, and a realization that what had just happened was deeply profound. Instantly, I just believed in God. Over the next few days I came to understand that he was now a factor in my life in a way that he had simply not been before. This was the start of my spiritual journey.

The remaining three stories in this chapter are all concerned with a calling to an ordained ministry. In the first story, Mary's sense of calling to ordination arises only out of the third occasion on which she hears a golden voice that has earlier in her life clarified whom she will marry and comforted her amidst distress. The voice that Gideon hears steers him away from accepting a post as a vicar in a parish that he later realizes would not have suited him. Finally, after a lifetime of service as a priest, Alan hears a voice that confirms him in his continuing ministry after retirement, and provides reassurance about what he is doing.

MARY'S STORY

I was brought up in a rather dysfunctional family, and became an easy target for a local paedophile (not my father). He abused me sexually for some time; I don't know how long, as for many years I suppressed the memories.

I moved away from my home town and met a lovely, kind and caring man. We went out a couple of times; exactly four weeks after our first date, I was alone at home and thinking of him, when a golden voice right inside my head said, 'You'll marry him, you know.' The voice wasn't at all frightening, simply warm and loving, and I believed it implicitly. The man and I have been married for quite a few years now. Whenever I tell people that I knew within a month that I would marry him, I don't mention the voice, because I don't want to be teased about 'hearing voices', whether I'm all right in the head, or other adverse comments.

In my early thirties, married and with a young family, I began to face up to the abuse. I was struggling towards faith, and my father was dying slowly of cancer. I went to sit in an unlocked church. It was completely empty or I would probably have left again straight away. I sat down and felt terrible, worthless and sad. Suddenly, the golden voice said to me, 'I love you, you know.' It sounded as though someone were leaning forward in the pew behind to speak to me. I turned round sharply to see who it could be, but the church was entirely empty. I knew it was God speaking to me, but I couldn't tell you how. Afterwards I started to find the courage to talk to a counsellor. Knowing I was loved by God was a revelation, as in my childhood he had always been a scary figure in the sky who only saw me to criticize and judge.

About 15 years after this incident, and now well settled in faith, I left my job in very bruising circumstances. At the same time, my husband's job had been threatened with redundancy. A week before he retired, my head of department told me that if I didn't buck my ideas up I would be out of a job. I had been working there for several years and despite plenty of opportunities, he had never brought it up before. In retrospect I know it wasn't true, but at the time I was devastated. After he left, the heads of other sections were asked to 'look after' me. Their advice was contradictory and amounted to bullying. I resigned a few months later. As part of coming to terms with this, I talked to our curate and when we prayed, God indicated that he had something good for me 'up his sleeve', and in 18 months I would know what it was. Some months, or maybe a year, later, in bed one night having a cup of tea before going to sleep, I dropped my bookmark on the floor. As I turned to pick it up, the golden voice said, 'You are the one I have ordained.' I turned to my husband and asked, 'What did you say?' He denied having spoken. In a panic, the next morning I talked to a friend in ordination training; after my disastrous vicarage childhood, ordination was the last thing I wanted. But God holds us on ropes of silk, and some years after that I was indeed ordained.

The golden voice was beautiful, melodious, kind and full of love. On the first occasion, I simply accepted it as true. There was no reason to disbelieve it, and anyway, it chimed with what I wanted! And it proved to be correct. When I was sitting in the church it filled me with a feeling of being wanted and loved, and that the dreadful childhood experiences could be redeemed. I think that's why it was 'golden', but it's very difficult to put into words. The last time, I simply knew it was the same voice.

Circumstances were very different but in the meantime I had learned a measure of trust in God. Other than these, I haven't heard God speak to me directly. When I prayed with our curate, the thought formed itself in my mind. Subsequently, I have found that if this happens when I am praying, whether alone or with others, that these are thoughts I can rely on and act on.

GIDEON'S[4] STORY

Some years ago [I] went through a trying time in my ministry. I had held two senior posts in the Church of England, but neither had been really right for me, and I eventually resigned from both. I found myself in the wilderness, spiritually and in terms of career. The Church had more or less written me off, and I was depressed and feeling alone. I prayed hard, and searched for a new job. Weeks went by and nothing emerged. Then someone suggested I apply for the incumbency of a key parish, then vacant. I wrote to the patron, but heard nothing back. I did my research on the parish. I continued to pray. I felt convinced that God was calling me to this new opportunity, and I looked forward to being appointed the new vicar. Nothing happened. In near desperation I asked God to show me what I should do. Would he intervene in the decision-making process? Then, a little later, on my knees praying, I distinctly heard a voice, which said, 'No!' It was a voice, not a thought, and it was very clear – almost in the room. It was an answer so sharp, I could not at first accept that it was God who was speaking to me: surely he would be more gentle and sensitive.

I was not offered the parish, but some time later I was invited to accept another important post, which I did, and was very happy doing. Ironically, when I retired from full-time parish life, the vicar of the former church asked me to join his staff as a pastoral assistant – which I was delighted to accept. I soon realized that I would have been completely the wrong person to have been made incumbent, and that God had chosen the right man for that role. I just had to learn to wait on the Lord with patience and humility.

4 Pseudonym.

ALAN'S STORY

I have always sought guidance in my life, but it certainly hasn't been immediately clear.

When a salesman I asked God whether I should change. Eventually, after two or three years, I can't remember exactly, I met my rector, thinking to talk with him about working with people, perhaps in probation, youth work or social work. He immediately put me into the machine that tests and then produces more fodder for the parochial ministry!! In the event, I have never doubted that I was in the right place.

Each move since has felt right, and I have served in five different parishes over 36 years. I have never felt I should go abroad or be in a specialist ministry.

Each year, since 1988, I think, I have availed myself of the opportunity afforded to those trained by King's College London of a three-day conference/retreat at Warminster, where we had our post-graduate training. I retired aged 66 in 2000 and booked in as usual. As was my custom every year, during the silent part of the retreat, I went for a jog up a local hill. Near the top I was praying – 'What now Lord?' I had been thinking that the important thing was to find out who I am, not being defined any longer by my role. Then, quite distinctly, I heard a voice that said, 'I have given you all the grace you need for what I want you to do.' Interestingly, the voice spoke not of who I am, but what I should do! Nineteen years on I am still being pastoral and taking services on the clergy rota!

I have not had any such encounter again.

Voices that confirm and clarify

Voices sometimes seem to answer implicit or actual questions arising from the contexts and crises of life, whether major or minor. Am I being selfish? Whom will I marry? Should I get divorced? Will things be okay? Am I on the right track? The uncertainties, anxieties and doubts surrounding such decisions can be significant, and it can be very comforting and reassuring to have a voice that confirms a course of action, affirms that things will be alright or clarifies what to do. In all of the stories reported in this chapter, future events seemed to confirm that the voice was right. At least, there is no reason to believe that what was confirmed or clarified was wrong. I did have one person contact me whose voice appeared to give the wrong advice. Sadly, I do not have their permission to include the story here. However, it is clearly not the case that voices are infallible, or that Christians always correctly identify whether or not a voice may be trusted. The hearing of a voice raises questions of discernment that will be addressed later, in Chapter 13.

Chapter 7

Companions

Voices are usually much more than just voices; they have social agency, they have personal characteristics, and they have identity. They are often associated with a sense of presence, so that people can talk of their voices being present even when they can't hear them.[1] Where they endure across a long period of time, they have history. They may thus become companions in life's journey and this companionship may take a variety of forms. I have included just two examples here, both of which are quite long, in order to give a feeling for the way in which the companionability of voices may operate across a longer period of time. I am not suggesting that either of these examples is 'typical' in any sense. Scientific studies of such voices appear to be very few, and I do not think it is possible to say what a typical example would look like (if, indeed, there is any such thing). Nor does there appear to be any normative historical or biblical model.

In the Judeo-Christian scriptures, the obvious example of a companion voice is that of the voice of God. Moses would seem to provide the most significant and striking example of a figure for whom the voice of God was an almost constant companion.[2] However, Moses is unusual. Whilst the companionship of God with many other biblical figures can be affirmed in a more general way, it is in most cases not clear that the voice of God was the primary mediator of this companionability. Even Jesus, as Son of God existing in a uniquely

1 For further discussion, see Cook (2018, pp.179–180).

2 Cook (2018, pp.61–62).

intimate relationship with the Father, is explicitly said to hear the voice of the Father on very few occasions.[3] When it comes to St Peter, St Paul or other apostolic figures in the early Church, we have no reason to believe that any kind of voice provided ongoing companionship.[4]

In Christian history, examples may be given of saints and angels, as well as divine voices, which provided ongoing companionship.[5] Thus, for example, Joan of Arc (c. 1412–1431) appears to have heard the voices of St Katherine of Alexandria, St Margaret of Antioch and St Michael the Archangel over a prolonged period of time. Maria Kowalska (1905–1938) experienced an ongoing inner dialogue with Jesus, sometimes hearing voices externally, over the course of many years. These examples are far from unique, but they are also far from typical. Companionship can take many forms, and the hearing of a voice is by no means essential to companionship with God. However, a voice (or voices) seems to be one of the forms in which it may be experienced.

ERROL'S STORY: GUIDED BY VOICES

My spiritual journey began the day I was born and eventually led me to a faith in God. My life seemed to be in black and white until, at the age of 21, schizophrenia coloured it in with colours no one could understand except me. I opened a door that I could never close and life flooded through in a way that chaos began to be interpreted by me as a way of life and other people understood it as a mental illness. This was the beginning of a transformation and what lay ahead was a struggle and the meaning of grace became clear as I trusted in a fate that was written by a divine hand. Hearing voices was a part of this new way of living and they appeared as visions as well as soft, sometimes enigmatic, concepts.

3 In the Synoptic Gospels, this is primarily at his baptism and at the transfiguration. In John's Gospel, when a voice from heaven is heard, Jesus says that it is for the benefit of the crowd and not for his sake (John 12.28–30). For a more detailed discussion see Cook (2018, pp.82–95).

4 There are, of course, instances where St Peter, St Paul and others did hear a voice, but this appears not to have been an ongoing affair (Cook 2018, pp.95–103).

5 Cook (2018, pp.110–144).

The care team came around to see me and my behaviour was a concern. I couldn't explain to them that my reality had a value that inspired me. All they could see was that I didn't fit into a neat little box labelled as 'normal'. They took me to hospital so they could observe me.

Gradually, my insight increased and I learned that there were things that I couldn't see but were very real. When I was in my flat after an episode of schizophrenia at the age of 23 I turned my thoughts to the invisible. On my knees praying to God for guidance was habitual for a complete year. It attracted voices. I was lost and confused. I needed direction and something to live for so I prayed that God would show me the way. It was repetitive and consistent and I was building up my faith by doing this. The voices were more than just hallucinations; they were like lights shining on the path in front of me. My grandmother used to say to me, when I was a child, that if ever I felt sad to pray to God and he would help me. I needed someone to show me the way because I was lost. I was walking barefoot with a diagnosis of schizophrenia with thorns strewn across the way and pits where deadly scorpions and poisonous vipers nested. [The voices] light shone with love and wisdom so I could see the traps of the enemy and thus avoid them. There are things that they seem to know and it has been proven to me time and time again that they can indeed see into the eternal endless vastness of time that is ahead of us. I can't understand why my companions, they are not just voices, know things about the future that I don't know and maybe I don't need to understand; instead I learned to trust them.

My voices didn't start with my descent into madness but gradually came to me as friends would come with water when I was thirsty. At times I had a thousand different messages coming from a thousand different voices in a variety of alien languages that I was translating into a new meaning. This meaning shaped my understanding and eventually led me to the waters of baptism. It took me 40 years of footsteps towards the waters of baptism and I was agnostic for many years, not really knowing if there was a God. But, through the darkness a light shone like a beacon for a lost sailor and I found my way home. Jesus said that we must get baptized and I was obedient to him because I loved him and his ways. It was then, after emerging from the waters, and empowered by the Holy Spirit, that I began to identify myself as a Christian.

The friendships that I have with my voices are real and I value them immensely. They are a comfort, and an encouragement to walk with Christ. God is the ultimate authority and to love him is a duty and a blessing. The thing about being receptive to hearing voices is that I am open to receiving the voices of guidance. My life has been shaped by prayer, faith and trust. In prayer I am participating in a communication with the most perfect, wise and loving God. He listens and he answers, sometimes in unexpected ways or through means that may not at first seem genuine. I have learned to not lean on my own understanding and to put into practice what I am taught or what I am instructed to do. When I prayed for direction of my life the answer, from one of my voices, was, 'I don't mind what you do as long as it is good.' This may seem quite simple but had a profound result. I started to look at life in terms of good and bad. It led me to question the influences that the world had on my way of life and I was evaluating things in a black and white approach. I began to see the harmful elements of negativity in music and television. I decided to try and live a life that would please God and that meant listening to the voices and working out what would please our Heavenly Father. We are taught to love him with all our heart, soul, mind and strength as well as our neighbour and ourselves (Mark 12.30–31). This royal law is the essence of Christian living. It is what my voices agree with.

Another time in prayer I asked for some advice and a male voice which seemed to be coming from a room where people were tapping away on keyboards in the background came across clear and meaningful. It said, 'Do not ridicule.' This left me with an insight into my own personality. I wondered at my propensity for wit and I realized that I use ridicule quite a lot in my humour. I never mean it to be hurtful but looking at it from a fresh perspective I began to see that it can at times be quite damaging towards other people who might be in a sensitive space. James 3.6 relates how the tongue is a fire, a world of iniquity. Bearing this in mind I have now become cautious of what I thought of as harmless fun. It may seem harmless to me but at the wrong time, wrong place and to the wrong person it can be quite painful. It is a pain that I would like to avoid so I have looked for other ways to express my appeal to laughter. It has led me to think a bit more often before I speak and also to reflect on what I have said to someone which might have been considered as crossing the line. If I think I might have offended someone I will make an apology and my voices will encourage me to do so.

Reflections on my life with voices...

Hearing voices comes in all sorts of guises and masks. In my experience, they seem to reveal what is deeply human about us and yet reflect our pain in such a way that we are left stunned by how real they are. Apart from their innate capacity to mirror our traumas they are also like angels. A tranquil voice in a time of anxiety brings peace to a troubled mind. It is like lighting a candle in the darkness. The angels are like messengers of harmony. They play the harp like when David plucked the strings to ease Saul's troubled soul to chase away evil spirits. And, in the darkness of the mind, they bring healing. At other times a voice might have other motives. There are demons disguised as angels and they only seek to mislead and confuse. Their motives are to separate us from God and draw us away from his paths of righteousness. They delight in pain and sin. Where these demons seek to possess us is in the wilderness of a barren heart. When we have the love of Christ they are momentarily silenced into incomprehension, but they still lurk in the shadows looking for a way to send fiery darts into our souls to wound and destroy. The angels come to the broken-hearted with healing messages of salvation and redemption. The evil spirits only seek to divide us whereas the angels always bring us closer to God and His almighty power and saving grace. There are ways to attract angels and this is by learning to serve Christ and obeying the Will of God. When you decide to commit yourself to the holy path of virtue, then things start to change. It seems like the powers of darkness are stronger and that there are so many demons trying to win a victory against the forces of good. It is these times that can be the most trying and sometimes I fail. But, when I have succeeded, I realize how close God is to me in these moments of adversity. He is there and even if I don't have the strength to fight, he always knows that I've tried.

There are so many ways a voice can affect my peace of mind that I become aware of shadows slipping in through the cracks of a broken conscience and forming shapes that are like ghosts but are made up of darkness. You can learn to sense evil and then find ways of dispelling the fear by learning to love completely. Voices respond to my inner emotional environment and it is perfect love that is my greatest weapon against the forces of darkness. I don't always love perfectly but to bring love into the arena where fear is wielding a terrible scythe of destruction can change the nature of my experience. Where voices are casting shadows of death on my soul the light of Christ shines. It is him that can save us. I need to not just listen to my still, small voice but also be guided by it in my daily life. I have tested it and tried out the instructions it has given me and it is worthy of leading me in the footsteps of Christ. All I lack is courage and faith. But, in a way, these are also my greatest strengths so that even if I fail sometimes I know that Heavenly Father has a plan for me. It might not make sense to a lot of people but my voices have led me deeper into the love of Christ so that the stars in the night sky are also the stars in my soul and they are there to guide me.

LUCY'S[6] STORY: IRON BUTTERFLY

The first encounter

I was born to a Buddhist family in the countryside of South Korea in 1978 when the majority of Koreans still suffered from poverty. My family was not an exception. I lived with my parents in a single, small room, until I was six years old.

One night, when I was four years old, I woke up without any reason, to find that my parents were both awake and looking at a bright light in front of the window. Within the bright light, a holy female figure called me to come to her. I could not hear any voice but just knew that she was calling me to come to her.

When I came to her, unexplainably I recognized that she had irresistible, great divine authority. I felt deep respect for her and tried to behave politely. At that moment, I felt some discussion was going on around us. (It was not a sound or voice. I just felt it was so. I sensed a change of energy or atmosphere.) I could not see them, but I became aware of many spiritual beings serving the holy, female figure. I believe

6 Pseudonym.

that they altered my consciousness in some way (beyond the limitations of a four-year-old girl), so that I could understand the situation. Then, she talked to me.

I perceived great and majestic authority from the figure, but her graceful, warm and kind attitude made me feel comfortable in her presence. She complimented me that 'You are a kind-hearted girl.'

I cannot remember anything after that. I do not know whether I simply forgot or for some reason the spiritual beings deleted my memory in some way. But, like a movie film which was deleted in the middle, I have no more memory after receiving her compliment. Since then, I occasionally felt frustrated because I knew that I received something crucial from the holy figure but I could not remember what it was. Interestingly, my parents could not remember anything of the episode at all. This encounter with the holy, spiritual, female figure became my secret.

I wonder now whether it was a dream? But, it was so vivid, and unlike other dreams, I can still remember well how I felt, the tone of her voice and warm compliments for me. While I was with her, I felt a deep peace and ineffable joy.

Spiritual hibernation

When I was about seven years old and at the elementary school, one day, I experienced what I would now call an altered state of consciousness on the long stair in front of my classroom. I became an observer, who somehow clearly penetrated my classmates' minds, who were playing in front of my eyes. I felt that I could comprehensively understand what was going on in this small society of human beings. I recognized their hatred, jealousy and carelessness, by which they caused complex and profound suffering to each other. At that time, I heard a graceful and thoughtful voice. It was like a gentle breeze. 'This is the world of human beings. How will you live?' I recognized the grave concern of the kind voice and the solicitous attitude toward me. Regrettably, I was scared due to the violent and cruel scene. Thus, immediately I answered that if someone hit me, I will hit them and if someone hurt me, then I will equally hurt them. After my answer, promptly my consciousness came back to the usual level, and I felt as though some spiritual protective energy was gone from me, and could not hear the kind voice anymore. However, I did not care about it at that time. I now feel that my answer was foolish and inappropriate, but I was young at the time and did not appreciate that then.

Several months later, one night before the date of an exam, I had a dream about an examination. Events transpired exactly as I had seen them in the dream. Except for these two episodes, I did not have any further spiritual experiences until I was 18 years old.

Turmoil in the grey dawn

After sitting a fiercely competitive entrance exam for medical school, physically and psychologically, I was extremely exhausted and felt unwell. To improve my health, I started to attend a popular Dahn Yoga centre. From the first class, I felt the subtle flow of Ki-energy between my palms and soon started to see the energy membrane (or aura?), surrounding human bodies, trees or mountains. I could distinguish good energy and bad (dark) energy by tactile sensation. The Dahn Yoga instructors explained the phenomena that I underwent with awe and wonder as the opening of the energy channels of my body, and expressed their embarrassment that this happened to me (a beginner) without significant effort.

These spiritual experiences broadened my worldview and completely changed my mindset. I was an atheist, and my only goal had been to be a successful professional to support myself independently. In other words, success in secular society was the only purpose of my life. Through these spiritual experiences, I started a spiritual journey to search for God and the ultimate truth, the meaning of life and death, and [the] afterlife.

Tragically, I soon became a target of various tempting voices, and the beings deserved to be called as 'evil spirits' and their tenacious attacks for possession. Their voices were extremely cunning and had several strategies. When I was strong, they often sent soft and tender voices to bolster my arrogant pride or anger. When I was weak, physically or mentally, some dominating voices penetrated my right temple with extreme pressure and tried to make me to commit suicide. When they tried violent attacks, sometimes I could see them visually – black moving beings like a black skein of thread. Gradually I intuited that their ultimate goal was to destroy my life, and also learned their strategies and methods: insulting and reminding me of my mistakes or deep inner wounds, whispering wrong or bad messages about situations or people, trying to stimulate my deep anger or wounds or to transfer dirty words and thoughts and sometimes extremely violent images or ideas with suicidal content.

Meditations were very helpful to try to figure out their goals and various strategies. As an observer of myself and the various evil voices, I carefully discerned the contents of what the voices said in order to selectively accept benevolent ones. I also learned that when I cannot distinguish whether a voice is benevolent or not, or whether it is true or not, the best policy is to ignore it. Then, I just followed my heart and the common sense.

Nevertheless, their attacks were growing more and more aggressive and vigorous. I finally admitted that it is impossible to protect myself by intellectual strategies and analysis anymore. Soon, I experienced possession. I felt another being in the right side of my head. It was a terribly scary moment. I desperately needed strong spiritual protection and help. In search of this, I explored many religious and spiritual traditions with deep sorrow and frustration. At last, in a small cathedral, I felt a strong connection and protection from Saint Mary (the mother of Jesus). When I prayed to her in a miserable state of mind, I felt deep peace and some images came to me – amidst bright lights, she was standing on a milky ground, and then, from the milky ground, an image of a dove came to me. I realized that the dove was coming to me from Mary. With deep prayers and dedication, I placed myself under the protection of Mary and Jesus. Gradually, prayers and golden lights from Mary expelled the evil spiritual beings, which had previously resisted so stubbornly.

Such experiences made me feel more isolated. I've been educated and trained in a radical medical materialism, which has forced me to keep my spiritual experiences secret, which cannot be told or shared with others for fear of not being accepted as a 'sane' member of society. This context significantly hindered me from exploring the deep spiritual meaning of my experiences.

Calling of my life

I graduated from medical school only through a process of overcoming the great inner turmoil that I was experiencing. During internship and residency, I encountered countless dying patients and their families. I profoundly experienced and shared psychological, existential and spiritual suffering with the dying, which gradually led me to contemplate the medicalization of death and to critically reflect on doctors' shallow understanding of death and death-denying modern societies.

After residency, although I had a good position as a fellow in the Endocrinology division, I somehow felt that this was not my way. My heart cried with torment, and I prayed devoutly for several months. Finally, I found the biography of Elisabeth Kübler-Ross: *The Wheel of Life*. I still remember the moment that I read her book in my dark little office. It was like being hit by lightning – an answer to my desperate prayers! I perceived it as a guiding message of the calling of my life.

Kübler-Ross's books and her courageous near-death studies greatly encouraged me. I became firmly convinced that to tell the truth of death is the calling of my life: death is just a transition, not extinction. I gradually started to prepare to study abroad to be a hospice doctor, thanatologist and death educator. Kübler-Ross's books played the role of a compass during the preparation period. Indeed, I received great consolation from her books because I felt that we have common ground. We are both female doctors who are profoundly interested in end-of-life care and existential and spiritual suffering around death and dying.

One day, while reading her biography again, I encountered the scene where she had experienced all the horror and agony of her patients' one thousand deaths 'to reaffirm the joy that came afterward'. At the end of all the suffering, she reaffirmed her faith in God and herself and had an out-of-body experience. She reached a beautiful spiritual realm where she heard the mysterious word, 'Shanti Nilaya', meaning 'the final home of peace' in Sanskrit.[7] From my heart, a strong voice rose, and I wrote (in Korean) 'I am an iron butterfly of God.'

7 Kübler-Ross (1998, pp.219–223).

Labyrinth and messages

Since I came to the UK, I started to attend a Quaker meeting and once participated in a Quaker retreat. In the early morning before the end of the retreat, I visited the labyrinth in the grounds of the retreat house. While walking the labyrinth, I received one invaluable message: 'Although you do not know where you are going in your life, like this labyrinth, your life has been well-planned already, and if you keep going on your path with the holy guidance, you will reach the centre (goal) of your life and smoothly exit from this material bodily life to another realm.' I bowed to show my sincere gratitude to the labyrinth.

As this episode in the labyrinth shows, receiving holy messages and guidance have been a major part of my inner life. In my experiences, as I understand them, the holy or evil messages (voices) do not come to my tympanic membrane as other sounds or voices do in this material world. The messages or ideas directly penetrate my brain or sometimes to my heart. Thus, it might be better to describe my experience as receiving holy energies, which I perceive as a message 'telling' me something. Sometimes I feel as if clear penetrating words come to me and [at] other times, it would be better to say that I recognize 'meaning' from holy energies. Such experiences are more distinct when I pray and receive golden lights from Mary and Jesus.

Prayer, golden lights and messages

Prayer is the core of my inner life. Whenever I feel drained of energy or depressed, I pray in front of my altar. When I focus on my heart and request help, I can see the beautiful and sacred golden lights around the statue of Mother Mary. Immediately after that recognition, I feel that a strong spiritual connection is made between Mary and me and the golden lights penetrate and surround my body for protection and healing. I often receive messages (voices, in Korean) during prayer:

> My beloved daughter.
>
> You are the chosen one.
>
> You will go to the way to God. Never worry about anything about your future. Just follow God's guidance.

> You are on the way to God and will always be guided and protected by God.

Recently, I began to sense a deep connection with Jesus, more precisely with his heart. When I pray in front of his picture, I can see the radiating golden rays from his heart, which connect between Jesus's heart and my heart. With this holy and blissful connection, my heart is full of joy and peace. I also sense that my state of consciousness is altered highly and feel greatly enlightened. Dark energies attached to my head, brain and shoulders flee away and my body experiences momentary shivers. I also see a golden aura surrounding Jesus. I presume that his holy energies are transmitting through the picture when I pray and messages (voices) are conveyed with the golden lights or messages (voices) come to me in the form of golden lights.

I have contemplated how I receive messages, particularly during prayer to Jesus and Mary. At first, I felt a great anxiety because I might give some incorrect interpretation or description about my spiritual experiences because of the two obstacles: (1) the ineffable nature of spiritual experiences which is hard to analyse or describe in [a] logical manner; and (2) the language barrier as a non-native English speaker. I deeply acknowledge that my work demands great prudence and responsibility because if I provide incorrect information, it might cause difficulties to other researchers studying human spirituality in depth. It makes me profoundly anxious and [it is] difficult to write more.

However, after a long observation and self-reflection, now, I think that I can say one thing. Because I found that the spiritual experiences during prayer are all about the 'golden light' from Jesus and Mary. When it comes directly to my brain, I accept it in a language form (Korean) as penetrating thoughts or words, but when it comes to my heart, immediately, my brain/mind is involved in making it in a language form. But, before making it as a language form, I think that my heart already knows what it means. The process of making messages in a language form is only to reveal the message (golden light) in a form that my logical mindset can understand, or it might be expressed that they move from sub-consciousness to consciousness. In other words, I feel that sometimes messages come directly into my consciousness and [at] other times they are infused into my heart or sub-consciousness so that the intentional efforts are needed to move them to a more conscious form, which can be understood, analysed and contemplated in my mind (brain). I cannot figure out what makes the two-different perceptions of messages from golden lights. What I know is that in my perception, it just happens in this way.

For instance, recently, due to over-drinking black tea, I experienced palpitation, chest tightness and dyspnoea. Thus, I had some fear of heart attack or early heart failure. Then, black energies approached me and told me that 'You will die soon. You cannot enjoy longevity.' In a depressive mood, I prayed to Jesus and felt that soft golden lights surrounded my heart with great love. My mind (brain) was involved in understanding the message, and made the message in a language form, 'Your heart will be fine. Your heart will be protected always. Never worry!'

Reflection about the interaction between various voices and my cognition or perception

Sceptics might argue that these messages (voices) are generated by my own brain. However, I can dispute such an argument with two reasons. Firstly, the holy messages (voices) are far beyond the level of my own thoughts or desires. To dedicate my life to God is the most strongly and frequently perceived message during my prayers to Mary and Jesus. This voice is directly opposing my basic desires such as safety, stability and social success for self-esteem. Thus, it was a difficult decision for me to quit my job as an endocrinologist and start to study palliative care and thanatology. Secondly, the characteristics of the voices, their colours and tones, are different to my own. Thus, when I receive messages (voices), as an observer, I keep cautiously discerning not only the contents of the messages, but also the colours and tones of the voices.

Great prudence and a cautious approach are needed when dealing with the various voices. Sometimes there is a danger even when receiving holy messages during prayer. The cunning evil beings furtively slide into my conversation with the holy voices. They often tempt me with sweet words to bolster my pride or desire for success, or introduce false wishes for the future. Thus, even during prayer and moments of receiving the holy voices with the golden lights, as an observer, I keep cautiously discerning the contents of the messages and the tone of the voices. I remember that the most trustworthy message is to dedicate and sacrifice my life to God. When I cannot distinguish the nature and intentions of the voices well, I just keep praying until everything is clear in my mind.

Companion voices

The two stories presented here are very different. What they have in common is a companionable experience of hearing voices that developed over time. In each case, this was integral to the growth and development of their Christian faith. Errol believes that his voices have led him into a deeper experience of the love of Christ. There are demons as well as angels, but he has learned to overcome the demons with love. Lucy's voices also take a malign form as well as a holy form, but she has learned how to discern the difference and how to manage the different kinds of message that they bring. It is her inner life of prayer, expressed in her relationships with Mary and Jesus, which has enabled her not simply to cope with her voices but also to find spiritual life in them. Both Errol and Lucy have found that their voices have provided guidance and direction in life.

Errol has received a psychiatric diagnosis, and Lucy has not. For some psychiatrists – and some theologians – this seems to be a very significant difference. It is suggested that the former is indicative of pathology, and that the latter implies an authentic spiritual experience. I feel strongly that this approach – a kind of differential diagnosis between psychopathology and 'genuine' spiritual or religious experience – is very unhelpful, and the stories offered by Errol and Lucy illustrate this nicely. This is not the place to rehearse the arguments for and against the utility of diagnostic concepts in relation to mental health generally, nor the validity of the particular concept of schizophrenia. I am aware that both are questionable, but I am happy to assume that the diagnosis is a correct and helpful one in Errol's case, not least because Errol himself finds it helpful. Others may take issue with me on this. Whether or not the diagnosis has been helpful, there has been a very real spiritual experience for Errol amidst the experiences labelled schizophrenia, and the label in no way invalidates these. Conversely, Lucy, like many others, hears voices but neither has nor needs any psychiatric diagnosis. Far from impairing her life and social functioning, Lucy's voices have enriched her life and enabled her to contribute to the wellbeing of those around her.

Both Errol and Lucy have reflected theologically on their experiences, and demonstrate a spirituality that is psychologically informed and self-aware. This interweaving of theology, spirituality and psychology has enabled them not only to cope but also to flourish. It has given them meaning and purpose in life. It has given them a tangible sense of companionship with a transcendent order.

Chapter 8

Communications

All intelligible voices are communications of some kind. Exactly what they communicate may or may not be reliable, meaningful or important. Thus, when in John's Gospel (10.1–20) Jesus, using (as the evangelist says) a 'figure of speech', refers to the sheep who know and listen to his voice, and the stranger whose voice they do not know, he is not suggesting that all Christians will 'hear voices'. Rather, the reader is invited to consider the ways in which Jesus (who in this Gospel is referred to both as the 'Word' of God, and also the good shepherd) speaks the truth, and can be trusted. His disciples will listen carefully for his voice (however that may be heard), and will be discriminating when presented with the voices of imposters. What Jesus has to say is reliable, meaningful and important. Not all voices have these qualities.

Christian scripture and tradition are replete with examples of voices that have been understood by Christians as revelatory. That is, they communicate something significant about God, or from God. Thus, Abraham is told that his offspring will be 'as numerous as the stars of heaven and as the sand that is on the seashore'.[1] In Luke's Gospel, the voice of an angel announces to Mary that she will conceive a son, who will be called Jesus. The voices at the baptism of Jesus, and at the transfiguration, are revelatory of Jesus's true identity. John has a visionary experience taking in all sensory modalities, including voices, which presents an apocalyptic panorama of what is to happen at the

1 Genesis 22.17.

end of time. Beyond the closure of the canon, Christian texts continue to provide similar and new accounts of revelatory voices. Francis of Assisi hears Jesus speak to him from a crucifix in a ruined church, telling him to rebuild his house. Julian of Norwich is told in a vision that 'everything has being through the love of God'.[2] And so we could go on.[3]

What has been communicated by these voices? They include important propositional assertions, some of the biblical examples of which are embedded in the very heart of Christian doctrine and teaching. They have also communicated things that have been personally and vocationally important to those who heard them – as in the case of St Francis, for example.

All of the voices reported in earlier chapters of this book have communicated something of personal significance to those who heard them. The six words that Keith heard in 1991 (see Chapter 2) have, according to his own account, been life-changing, giving him cause to reflect on what it means to 'come home' and enabling him to find purpose in life. When Ravi heard a voice telling him to 'go where the sky is black' (Chapter 3), the interpretation of what was communicated was highly contextual, being closely related to his thinking about the possibility of a vocation to a ministry in a country parish. It also had layers of meaning, being more deeply concerned with the light that Christ would bring amidst darkness, wherever he chose to serve. Margaret's voice (Chapter 4) communicated information about where she would find the step under the water that would prevent her from

---

2 Colledge, Walsh and LeClercq (1977, p.183).

3 See Cook (2018) for references and for numerous further examples and critical analysis. I am not concerned here with such historical-critical questions as to the historicity of Abraham, or the nature of the psychological experiences of the historical Jesus, but rather with the significance of the inclusion of such stories in the canon of scripture that has been handed down within the Christian tradition. Whatever the historical and psychological realities behind the text, these stories are included in Judeo-Christian scripture, and thus provide a significant scriptural precedent for the idea that voices communicate propositional content that is reliable, meaningful and important.

drowning. The voice that Judith heard (Chapter 5) communicated compassion not so much by what was said as by the way in which it was said. In Chapter 6, several stories relate experience of voices that communicated guidance on what decisions should be made amidst uncertainty about what to do. In Chapter 7, the voices that Errol and Lucy heard were found sometimes to be reliable, and sometimes not, and they both found that they had to learn to distinguish between the two. What was communicated by the good voices was important for each of them personally.

Some voices have a wider impact, being significant not only for the person hearing them, but also – at least eventually – for wider society. Figures such as Francis of Assisi, Joan of Arc, Florence Nightingale and Teresa of Calcutta changed the course of history. What was communicated to them concerning their own vocations directly and indirectly changed the lives of those around them. Similarly, even if not as widely known, Ravi's voice has had an effect on the life of a whole parish in Kent, who would not otherwise have had experience of his ministry. In Chapter 5, Lucy reported an account of a voice that communicated comfort to others, and not only to her, even across boundaries of religious difference.

I include in this chapter three stories that provide accounts of communication on a particular theme – the theme of suffering. Whilst these are all very personal experiences, they have wide significance for those reporting them in terms of their Christian faith, their relationships with God and their relationships with those around them. The first of Ellen's two stories does not include a voice, but the communication that it concerns is anchored in a sense of the presence of the suffering Christ. Her second experience, only a month later, which includes a phenomenologically interesting account of voice hearing, is concerned with the suffering of those around her. In Willelmina's case, the voices that she hears have significance reaching back historically to her roots of origin and outwardly in her sense of belonging to a people who have suffered deeply.

ELLEN'S STORIES[4]

Strange beauty

I went to a concert with a friend at Wigmore Hall in December 2016, having flown in from the US that morning. I was tired but had had a long nap, so felt fairly good. I was looking at the painting above the stage and just listening to the music. Suddenly reality faded away and I was looking at the naked, dead body of Christ – but just the hip and upper thigh. There was strong light on it like a sunrise, and the rest was in grey mist. It was beautiful – the skin was white and luminous. And there was a perfume, like carnations or more specifically, dead human flesh, but not unpleasant. It felt like I was being made to understand pain and suffering – the nature of it – somehow. This was unusual both because of the smell and also because of the presence of Christ. None of my experiences up to that time had had Christ feature so explicitly before. On coming to, there was a sort of 'reordering' of my relationships with people in my mind, as well as a kind of renewed sense of purpose in myself.

Suffering on an aeroplane

Another experience happened on a flight back from holiday in Spain in January 2017. I'd been to see the church/mosque in Cordoba and also to the Alhambra. It was a great trip, but I was tired – I'd been ill with food poisoning the night before the flight. I poured myself into my seat and put my headphones on, listening to Arvo Part's 'The Deer's Cry' on repeat, to unplug. I drifted off to sleep briefly. When I awoke, I felt odd. I turned the music off and took my headphones off. Suddenly it was as though I could hear the thoughts of the people on the aeroplane – the closest thing I can liken it to is tuning an old-fashioned radio, when as the dial turned there was a lot of static and sometimes multiple stations would come through at once. This is what it 'sounded' like, although much like the Barcelona experience, I was not hearing this with my ears. It was like music – layers of meaning expressed through different voices. What came through was deep suffering as an element of the human

4 An earlier experience of Ellen's, which she refers to here as the 'Barcelona experience', is reported in Chapter 6.

condition. People were worried about all sorts of things, things they'd left behind before they boarded, things they were going to land into, the fact that they were flying in an aeroplane, and just the random things that make up a life. They were waves of anxiety and pain, and it had a sort of terrible beauty about it. I was mesmerized. Then I made a mistake – to try and 'grab' onto it – and it faded. The experience had a profound impact on me – previous experiences had been more about individual suffering, while this was more of an awareness of suffering being a part of the warp and weft of what it means to be human. It still amazes me.

WILLELMINA'S STORY

I am an African Caribbean. In 2005 I travelled to Ghana with my sister. I had already been diagnosed with bipolar disorder for several years. When we visited Elmina Castle on the coast, my sister and I both heard the voices of people screaming when we paid fees to enter. (Elmina is a former fort and holding station for Africans awaiting shipment to the Americas.) We both responded simultaneously with the same words. We both said, 'But we've already paid!' Later, on entering the women's cells and on being shut in, I heard the voices again – women's voices, wailing and screaming. I came home with those voices. For my sister, it was a one-off experience, but for me, it has continued. Whenever I get stressed or upset the voices increase in volume and emotion. As the voices began in that place, I understand the voices as coming from ancestors who have found a conduit in me as I was vulnerable. It has taken a few years to come to this understanding because I first thought that I was possessed.

I hear the voices all the time. They are always with me in the background. They are like conversations you hear in the background. They are there even when I am happy. The voices are affected by prayer – they become quieter when I pray the rosary. At Mass they become a whispering sound in the background and when praying at home, as long as I'm calm, they are unintrusive (almost respectful). They are loudest at night and they often wake me up. I used to be frequently in tears until I began to honour them; they still do induce tears sometimes, especially at night.

> I pay attention to my ancestors now even as a Roman Catholic. I acknowledge them at family events by pouring libations and I keep a special place in my home where I keep objects that connect me with my ancestors and remind me of my African culture. Some might call this a shrine!

Voices as communications

The three experiences presented here are very different, even though two of them are reported by the same person. Ellen's experience of the presence of Christ does not exactly include a voice, but has a noetic, mystical quality by way of which she comes to understand the 'nature' of suffering. This is deeply personally significant for her, bringing about a 'reordering' of her relationships and priorities. Only a month later, this same concern with suffering emerges in an experience aboard an aircraft, this time being focused on the contemporary suffering of her fellow passengers. Their sufferings are almost literally given voice in her experience. We might say that the first experience is Christocentric, whereas the latter experience locates similar concerns in the contemporary human context. What has been communicated? Ellen has learned nothing that she didn't know previously. She was aware of the Christian story of Christ suffering for humankind. She was aware, in a general sense, that people all have their own troubles. However, through these experiences she gained a new personal understanding of the nature of suffering. Her perspective on suffering, her own, that of other people and especially that of Christ in relation to others, had changed.

Willelmina's experience was also a very personal one, and also reaches out to others around her. Unlike Ellen, Willelmina has been diagnosed as suffering from a mental disorder, but it would be foolish to take this as a reason for dismissing her voices as meaningless. On the contrary, they are deeply meaningful. The immediate experience is shared with her sister, but this experience is also a wider sharing with her ancestors and an identification with her African roots, historically, culturally and spiritually. As in Ellen's case, what has been communicated is not new information so much as a new awareness of her own belonging to a wider web of human suffering, and a new sense of the relationship between this and her Christian faith.

Given what we now know about the relationship between voices and trauma,[5] it is perhaps not surprising that many of the stories in this book concern suffering of one kind or another. However, the links that Ellen and Willelmina make between their voice-hearing experiences and their experiences of suffering are not direct or straightforward. They reach out to identify with the experiences of suffering of other people around them, and they seek to put this suffering in a theological and spiritual context, but they do not relate directly to the biographical narratives of childhood trauma or any other personal suffering.

The propositional content of what voices communicate can be significant, but it is not the only thing that matters, or necessarily the most important thing. Presence, the identity or compassionate tone of the voice, context and a certain kind of ineffable impact on the hearer, may all be more important than what is actually said. Not all voices tell the truth, but the communications that voices convey can be spiritually and theologically, as well as psychologically, significant.

5 See, for example, Daalman *et al.* (2012).

Chapter 9

Conversational Prayer

Some voices have a conversational quality to them. That is, there may be a dialogue between the voice and the person hearing the voice. Where the voice is understood to be God's voice, the conversation may be construed as prayer. It is a kind of prayer which has an Old Testament model in narratives concerning God's relationship with Moses and Abraham, amongst others.[1] There seems to be no precisely similar account in the New Testament, although Ananias has a brief dialogue with God in Acts 9, and Peter has a dialogical exchange with a heavenly voice in Acts 10 (as does Cornelius, with an angel). Jesus has a dialogue with Satan in the wilderness, and John has something like a dialogue with various heavenly figures encountered in his vision in Revelation.

Later Christian tradition provides a variety of examples of conversational prayer. There is a dialogical quality to the voices that Julian of Norwich (c.1342–1416) hears in the course of her visions and her younger contemporary, Margery Kempe (c.1373–1438), describes frequent dialogical exchanges, both with God and with various saints. Ignatius of Loyola (1491–1556), founder of the Jesuit order, includes colloquy, a kind of prayerful conversation, in his spiritual exercises. He explains that:

1 Cook (2018, pp.57–62).

> A colloquy, properly so called, means speaking as one friend speaks with another, or a servant with a master, at times asking for some favour, at other times accusing oneself of something badly done, or sharing personal concerns and asking for advice about them.[2]

In the 20th century, Gabrielle Bossis (1874–1950) and Maria Kowalska (1905–1938) provide examples of conversational experiences of prayer within the Roman Catholic tradition. Conversational prayer becomes especially prominent, however, in recent times in some protestant evangelical traditions. Joyce Huggett, in *Listening to God*, a book that has been highly popular since first publication in 1986, gives a number of examples of this kind of prayer. She places the emphasis, as the book's title suggests, on what God has to say to her, rather than on what she has to say to him:

> What I heard in those times of listening was more than a voice. It was a presence. Yes. I heard the Lord call my name. But I also 'heard' his tenderness. I soaked up his love. And this listening was on a level which runs deeper than mere words. Sometimes it seemed as though Jesus himself stood in front of me or beside me or above me. This encounter with him overwhelmed me.[3]

Huggett's approach to prayer has many of the qualities of a more contemplative spirituality that, as this quote suggests, often goes beyond the purely verbal. In other cases, however, there is much more focus on the words, and on the familiarity of conversational exchange. Tanya Luhrmann has undertaken extensive research on this kind of prayer, as reported in her book, *When God Talks Back*.[4]

The following three accounts provide examples of how such conversational approaches to prayer may be experienced.

---

2 Ivens and Hughes (2004, p.21).

3 Huggett (1986, p.33).

4 Luhrmann (2012). See also research based in the UK by Dein and Cook (2015) and Dein and Littlewood (2007).

KLAIR'S STORY

Since I became a Christian, six years ago, I have been talking to God and hearing God's voice. Not knowing any better, when I started going to church I thought most Christians heard God when they prayed and I started to get confused about that, as I thought if they had been going to church for years they would know all about it! I went on a guided Retreat at St Beuno's in North Wales and talked to a guide there, rather worried that I might be going mad, hearing voices, but he reassured me that the whole idea of the Ignatian exercises in prayer is to practise listening for God's voice and having dialogue with God. Since then I have managed to find a number of other prophetic Christians who hear God's voice in a variety of ways, and we now share with each other what we hear – which is often the same thing! Some of them receive pieces of scripture, which has been rare for me because I don't know the Bible as well as they do, though God sometimes gives me a modern parable in response to a question I've asked – I don't always understand them! I am now doing an Authorized Lay Ministry course through the diocese of Worcester as an evangelist, talking to more people about prayer and having a personal relationship with God.

In the beginning, when I didn't know how to pray and could not bring myself to go into a church (I had been a rather militant atheist for years), I decided to use meditation techniques to picture myself in a chapel (kind of like those exercises where you imagine building your dream home), and the first time I did this I was aware that I wasn't alone in the chapel I'd created; there was a man there, dressed in a clerical suit, maybe in his forties, blonde; not like anyone I recognized. He sat down next to me and said, 'You've got questions. Ask your questions.' I said I wanted to pray but didn't know how, and so he began to speak these prayers, that sounded like ones a priest might say, only I knew I didn't know them!! After a few days of going into this chapel for prayer time and having him pray with me, I asked him what I should call him and he said, 'Companion'. At the time I did wonder, as I said, if I was losing the plot altogether, but much later, when I became a volunteer in the diocesan library, I found books that documented other instances incredibly similar to mine, especially that of Catherine Marshall, who also called her accompanier 'Companion'. I have come to believe that this is the way in which the Holy Spirit comes to me, as a Companion on the journey, and to begin with his was the voice I heard and I experienced him as being very much with me in daily life and not just inside the imagined chapel. I talk to him and ask him to explain things about faith I don't understand.

Companion 'talks' to me, as a voice in my thoughts, but I also have the sense of his presence, often walking alongside me, like a friend would. In some circumstances this has been very clear. On one occasion, weeding in the churchyard, a young black man came and asked me for help and wanted to go into the church to pray but wouldn't go in unless I went with him. Suddenly standing at the back of the church, I found myself thinking, 'What if he's got a knife or something in that bag he's just taken off his shoulder?!' Companion felt like a very strong presence standing next to me saying, 'It's alright, you're not on your own, it'll be fine.'

Later I also began to experience a voice I associate with God as Father, and this is a voice inside me, like audible thoughts. When we are talking and during times when he is trying to communicate something important, I also receive pictures along with the words, which are often memories, that seem to be there to help me to interpret how to take what is being said through association and the emotion they evoke. I do also hear Jesus, though it is usually during Mass.

The Ignatian exercises encourage dialogue with various figures, but especially Jesus, and when I was doing those imaginative prayers, I did have dialogues with him, and for a while afterwards, but it feels like, where I am on my journey right now, the Father is more what I need and that's why I think I hear God more often as a parent. When God speaks to me all I can say is that it is a different voice than Companion's voice (my parish priest used to be a psychiatric charge nurse and he does assure me that I am NOT crazy!) and they have different ways of telling me things. Their voices are always inside my thoughts, yet I know they are not my 'own' thoughts. I ask questions and I get answers and sometimes the answers are astonishing and not anything that I could've made up myself.

KIT'S STORY

Like all clergy, I accepted that God speaks to people through scripture, His peace (or lack of it), other people, impressions, prophecy, etc., but it was only in about 1990 I realized that God could (and wants to!) speak directly to me. This revelation was occasioned by the visit of two remarkable Christians (now both dead) to our church for a ministry weekend. They were Iolo and Freda Hughes. Through their ministry, I realized God wanted to speak to me personally. Up till then, the story of God speaking to the boy Samuel, and the words in John's Gospel, 'My sheep hear my voice', had just somehow passed me by!

So, I began to ask God to speak to me, as I prayed, and, sure enough, I heard His voice (I believe) speaking to my mind, and this has continued to this very day. It just seems to be so natural – as it says in Ephesians, 'Through Christ we have access to God.' What to me is simpler than that?! (I hasten to add, though, that I have never heard an audible voice.)

So things went on from there. I realized, of course, that Satan can try to get a hold on me, and that many people have heard malevolent voices, so I always discount any voice that is not consonant with the Word of God, as revealed in the New Testament. I find, too, the voice of God is never strident, always kindly – even if occasionally telling me off! The voice, too, is always in modern vernacular, never in archaic, or BCP [Book of Common Prayer] English. Of course, I have wondered whether I was hearing just my own thoughts, so I said to God, 'God, am I just talking to myself?' The reply came back, 'Do I sound like you talking to yourself?!' The answer was 'No', from me.

Someone once said, 'The Holy Spirit is a gentleman, and waits to be asked.' And that's my experience too. He doesn't butt in, so I have time in my prayers to say to him, 'What have you to say to me, Lord, today/ about this situation/regarding tomorrow's event?'... Etc., etc.

(Having said that, I did experience one time when God did butt in, unasked for. It was when, in my fifties, I was playing squash with my younger son. It was a hard-fought game, and the score was 2–2 in games, and 9–9 in the fifth game. I was tired but knew that, in squash, you have to win by two clear points to win a game. It was then that I heard God say clearly, 'That's enough Kit', and we called it a draw. I wonder, since, if God was saving me from a heart attack.)

When I ask God to speak to me, I receive beautiful encouragements and guidance. For example:

> I love you to bits.
>
> I look forward to your praying.
>
> I'm the Lord of the Universe, but the gentlest person you'll ever meet.
>
> When I've been unsure of doing something, I've heard him say, 'I wouldn't do that, if I were you.'
>
> Sometimes, asking advice on very mundane things, I receive words like, 'You'll be okay, Kit', or 'Don't worry, I'm with you.'

I occasionally have a vision, but mainly words. (Maybe God knows I'm not a very imaginative person. Buying presents is always a headache!)

Sometimes, the Lord does correct me, with words like, 'That wasn't a good idea, yesterday, to do (x) or (y)', or 'You need to apologize.'

When I ask him to show me my sins to repent of, he verbally reveals the bad trends in my nature, of which surface sins are the outcome.

JULIA'S STORY

I am not sure quite how to describe what is a long history of conversations with God and visual prompts over many different occasions, most of them of an everyday nature. These are all quite different from my talking to myself or even the conversations that I have had with myself via what I would term imaginary friends. The encounters with God speaking to me are more memorable and stand out.

I can recount times when God called me to follow him which led to me offering myself for ordination. This began when I was 18 at an event at Lee Abbey. At the time I was not that immersed in Christian belief. I was alone after a seminar and God asked me to commit my life to him. I was shocked and just turned away. This was in the 1960s. Later, although being very involved in church over many years, it wasn't until the late 90s that I heard God asking me to do more for and with him. So I went to an event to hear about vocations, thinking of being a reader, and God said 'NO! I want you to be ordained.' Again I was somewhat reluctant, but once I accepted that call I heard a voice saying, 'You are loved.' The process of training and serving has not always been what I expected, but each time I stepped out in faith and responded to opportunities I have found that God has gone before me.

A recent example may help to give a flavour of my experiences. On one occasion, I was walking along a road in the built-up area where I live and it was cold but not wet and a voice told me to take off my shoes and stand on the cold pavement. I resisted at first, thinking this was not something that I should be seen doing. The command was repeated so I obeyed. Then, as the cold was felt for a minute or so, the voice said 'You will remember this.' I then thought of Moses and the burning bush. Every place can be Holy ground. I have shared this appropriately in sermons and groups as a witness to God being alive and speaking to us in everyday life. It illustrates that we need to trust and obey.

There have been many other small prompts, each of relevance to me and a reassurance of God's presence in Christ in my life through the Holy Spirit, even when I was far off. It is quite difficult to write about these experiences. In some public media they can be sources of ridicule or even darker judgements.

As regards the experience of God's voice, it is authoritative, but not authoritarian, familiar, recognizable and trustworthy, like that of a friend/mentor. I experience it as clearly coming from outside myself and have always understood it as being aloud but not necessarily heard by others, although as I am generally alone and not in a public place, who is to say? All these experiences are quite intimate and personal and yet Christian literature describes a number of people who have experience of God in conversation with them (the *Imitation of Christ* by Thomas à Kempis, for example),[5] so I have always regarded talking with God as part of my life. As one hymn says, 'I serve a living Saviour he walks with me and talks with me along life's narrow way.' These daily conversations are different from the times which are rarer when God speaks aloud from outside, as with the call to ordination or the incident (above) that involved taking off my shoes.

5 See Sherley-Price (1952).

Daily conversations with the Lord are different in tone, they are more like talking to a friend, often taking the form of a prompt to go and visit someone. So, for example, in the case of contacting a passing acquaintance, I really felt it would be intrusive on my part, yet when I made contact there was a real need there of grief and sadness. The response from God is more like 'I told you this was right. Why do you doubt my advice?' On other occasions God asks me to ring someone and when they answer they often say, 'I was just thinking of you!' Other times, when I am with people, God prompts me to ask or say something and I am surprised by saying things that I didn't know that I knew.

Equally usual examples are about any anxieties, or worries, that I have. The conversation can end with the Lord saying 'STOP fretting! I will now deal with that', and he does, especially when I am worried about a particular relationship or situation, including family ones.

All these conversations are very difficult to make explicit as they are like talking to a friend and are often fleeting and sometimes quite ordinary, often more like a stream of consciousness, but with the Lord, not with myself.

As regards my other internal voices, the imaginary friends who are more like a family, these have been familiar with me from a very early age and continued through my adult life. They are friendly, interested in me, and help me to make sense of life as well providing a wry commentary on events and being someone to talk to when things are boring. I can, of course, provide a rationale for this particular aspect of my internal life which has never really been shared with friends or family.

I am pleased to read that you are regarding some of this as normal, but I would emphasize that the voice of God is different and always memorable whereas my conversation with my other internal voices passes and fades. I would wish it known that Christ is alive, and speaking with him is a normal and encouraging part of Christian life and not something exceptional, except for the fact that any contact with God is sacred and special and not to be taken lightly. We stand on Holy ground when we are with him.

I have noticed since our email exchanges [a year ago] that the voices, both personal and the ones from God, have been less and muted.

However, that may be more due to being distracted by family and church matters, although God's presence has always been around me.

Prayer as conversation with God

Klair's story begins with an imaginary encounter with 'Companion'. The voice of Companion, whom she now understands as being the Holy Spirit, is in her thoughts, rather than being out loud, but it is accompanied by a sense of presence. She distinguishes this from 'a voice inside me, like audible thoughts', whom she identifies as God the Father. This is a visual and affective experience, and not merely a voice. Her encounters with Jesus are associated with a more sacramental context, or when engaged in Ignatian meditational exercises. Like Margery Kempe in the 14th century, Klair's conversational encounters with God are Trinitarian. Whilst they are all in her thoughts, she is clear that they are not her own thoughts. Although Klair herself does not draw attention to this, her experience is evocative of the words of Isaiah:

> For my thoughts are not your thoughts, nor are your ways my ways, says the Lord. For as the heavens are higher than the earth, so are my ways higher than your ways and my thoughts than your thoughts. (55.8–9)

Similarly, although Kit's conversations with God are in his mind, when he asks, 'God, am I just talking to myself?', the reply 'Do I sound like you talking to yourself?!' evokes an emphatically negative response. Julia distinguishes God's voice not only from her own thoughts but also from imaginary friends with whom she has conversed since childhood. Her encounters with God are 'more memorable'; they 'stand out'. God's voice is 'authoritative…familiar, recognizable and trustworthy'. Unlike Klair and Kit, Julia also experiences God's voice as coming from outside herself, and describes it as 'aloud', although she also recognizes that it would probably not be heard by others.

Klair initially worried that she might be 'going mad', and Julia expresses concern about ridicule or judgemental attitudes from others. Whilst these concerns are completely understandable, it is interesting that they arise in relation to experiences which – as voices – are phenomenologically common within the general population, and – as prayer – are normative amongst many Christians and churches (as Tanya Luhrmann's research shows).[6] These concerns appear to reflect, on the one hand, the lack of public understanding of the nature of voice hearing and, on the other hand, a worry about being associated with a tradition of Christianity that is sometimes perceived by the media as extreme or odd. In fact, it is clear that such experiences are neither odd nor uncommon.

Simone Weil suggested that, 'Attention, taken to its highest degree, is the same thing as prayer. It presupposes faith and love. Absolutely unmixed attention is prayer.'[7]

If we are fully attentive to the voices within, then who is to say that God may not speak to us through them? On the other hand, as Kit suggests, voices may also be malevolent or deceptive, and so there is a need for discernment. Most Christian traditions within which conversational approaches to prayer have become normative have therefore also devised critical approaches to discernment.[8] The question becomes not so much 'Do we hear God in prayer?' as 'How may we know that it was God?' Some Christian traditions of prayer emphasize more the wordlessness of prayer, the unknowability of God and the dangers of deception. Others, as exemplified here, emphasize more the importance of loving attentiveness to divine speech. It is surely a strength of Christian spirituality that it is able to embrace this diversity?

6 Luhrmann (2012).

7 Weil (1952, p.117).

8 Cook (2018, pp.125–126); Huggett (1986, p.145); Luhrmann (2012, pp.62–67). See also Chapter 13, this book.

Chapter 10

Conversational Voices

Most of us experience our thoughts as inner voices. When we read silently, we can 'hear' the words in our heads. When we prepare what we will say at an important meeting, we do not need to say the words out loud; we can rehearse them internally. Inner speech is, however, not quite the same as what we say out loud. In particular, it is condensed or contracted, so that we don't have to say all of the words in full. Nonetheless, it is still verbal. Psychologists believe that this inner speech is an internalized version of social speech, which we learn at an early age in conversation with our parents, siblings and others. Because it is learned in dialogue with others, our inner voices have an inherently dialogical nature. There is more than one voice.

Usually, we own both parts of this inner conversation as being our own thoughts, but in order to have such a conversation at all, we have to be able to distinguish between the dialogue partners. The psychologist Charles Fernyhough[1] refers to this ability to identify an inner dialogue partner as an 'open slot' into which we can place another perspective and then dialogue with it. Thus, I can imagine the conversation that I might have with my boss, when I tell him that I am not happy with how he treated my application for promotion. (I might never say these things, of course, but I can imagine the conversation!) As a child,

1 Fernyhough (2016).

I might use this capacity to generate conversations with an imaginary playmate. In fact, children who have imaginary companions seem to have a better internalization of private speech than those who do not.[2] I can thus dialogue internally with an imaginary conversation partner who is not me.

There is another characteristic of our inner voices, however, which complicates things further. When I speak out loud, I can decide in advance what I want to say. In a hasty moment, I can say something that I regret, but it was still 'me' that said it. Inner voices, on the other hand, can simply arise spontaneously and without my conscious bidding. Indeed, as is widely known, trying not to think about something is the surest way to find yourself thinking about it! It is very difficult to think about nothing. Thoughts arise spontaneously, from we know not where. A psychoanalyst might argue that they come from our unconscious mind, and that they reveal things about our deepest concerns. A Christian (or other religious person) might argue that they sometimes come from God. Indeed, there is a tradition of arguing that God speaks to us through our unconscious,[3] and so these two ways of thinking are not necessarily incompatible. The striking thing is that thoughts come into my mind that I did not intentionally put there. I might not even want them there. I might strongly wish to disown them – but they are there.

The philosopher Daniel Dennett (not known for his sympathy for religious belief) has described consciousness as a pandemonium.[4] Our minds are filled with all kinds of thoughts that might originate from all kinds of different places. Dennett has a variety of terms to describe this pandemonium, but one of them strikes a cord with early Christian spirituality. They are 'word demons'. They come unbidden, as though from outside our minds; they emerge into our consciousness, and then they depart. In fact, these demons need not be bad. Evagrius, one of the early Christian Desert Fathers, suggested that our thoughts might come from demons, but they might also be angelic, or they

2 Davis, Meins and Fernyhough (2013).
3 Bomford (1999).
4 Dennett (1991).

might simply be human thoughts, emerging from our own minds. The problem is telling the difference, given that we have a strong propensity to fool ourselves about our own motives. Thus, I might like to think that my thoughts about gold are good, because I want to give to the poor, when in fact they reflect the avarice that is deep within my heart.

What does any of this have to do with the voices that Christians hear? I think it is important for a number of reasons. Most importantly, it reminds us that consciousness is complicated, and that we do not always know where voices come from. When we pray, for example, all kinds of things might come into our heads. Perhaps they are from God, but perhaps they are not? Perhaps they are just mundane distractions that are neither good nor bad, such as the sudden awareness that I forgot to phone the dentist to cancel my appointment! It is easy to want to simplify things, and easy to be over-confident about our own ability to identify thoughts as demonic or divine, but actually, if we are honest, we often do not know where they come from. Happily, not knowing where they come from is not as bad as we may fear.

When the thoughts that come into our heads seem as though they are not 'ours' – that I would never have thought such a thing – that is certainly interesting. It reflects our mental capacity to hold a dialogue with an imagined partner who is 'not me'. However, it does not actually prove where the thought came from. Perhaps it is a meaningless part of the mental pandemonium? Perhaps it is divinely inspired? Perhaps it tells me something significant about myself? There are competing psychological theories that one can adopt to make sense of such experiences, and there are competing Christian spiritualities. Early Christian wisdom would suggest that (at least initially) being attentive to these thoughts, aware of them but not overly attached to them, seems to be the best way to deal with them. As we get to know their comings and goings better, we learn better how to deal with them.

The stories included in Chapter 9 illustrate a positive Christian spirituality, within which thoughts that seem to come from God can, with appropriate discernment, be included as conversation partners in prayer. Other Christian spiritualities, those that are more apophatic, take a radically different approach. As much as possible, they eschew words. As I indicated in Chapter 9, there are ways of combining elements of both approaches, such as Joyce Huggett's influential book, *Listening to God*, which takes something of a middle path. It is not my intention here to critique these different spiritualities, but rather to note that they each provide their own responses to how Christians may effectively manage their inner voices in prayer.

Inner voices also become important in the context of psychotherapy, counselling and engagement with mental health services. Whilst, in principle, I do not think that this should pose any problem for Christians, in practice, it often does. These problems arise, in part, as a result of the 'religiosity gap', whereby mental health practitioners, who are more likely than their patients to be atheist or agnostic, do not always understand the Christian language of prayer.[5] When someone says 'God told me…', this can easily be misdiagnosed as evidence of psychopathology. Happily, there is increasing awareness amongst mental health professionals of the need to address such potential misunderstandings in a more person-centred and respectful fashion.[6]

However, psychological therapies can still present complex, controversial and theologically challenging dilemmas in a realm of experience that is, at the same time, both psychological and spiritual. The story that I am including in this chapter is, in many ways, unusual. It concerns a diagnosis of dissociative identity disorder, which is probably the most controversial mental health category of current diagnostic systems. I do not wish to enter into the debate here as to its nature and origins.[7] Whatever they may be, the following account vividly shows how an inner conversation can at the same time generate important psychological and spiritual challenges, with the potential for good or bad outcomes.

DOMINIC'S[8] STORY

On 23 February 2011, I discovered that I have DID, or dissociative identity disorder, which was formerly (and unhelpfully) known as

5 Cook (2011a).

6 See, for example, Cook (2013b); and Royal College of Psychiatrists (2018).

7 Reinders (2008).

8 Pseudonym.

multiple personality disorder. Clearly, this was a bit of a shock! Especially as I was thousands of miles from home, deep in the Australian Bush, at the time.

I had gone there to attend a course for adult survivors of childhood trauma and abuse and, halfway through the week, had the extraordinary experience of my body being 'taken over' by someone or something else. One minute I was lying on the ground crying; the next I had been flipped over by this alien force and was walking on all fours but facing upwards – like Linda Blair in the infamous spider-walk scene in *The Exorcist*, an appropriate analogy because, as a Christian, I assumed that what was happening was some sort of demonic possession. However, I quickly realized that this was not the case when the facilitator who was with me asked me what was happening and someone else answered her, but using my mouth!

I suppose it could have been a demon but somehow I just knew that it wasn't and I'd read enough about DID to recognize it when I saw it. Again, a sceptic could say that this was auto-suggestion, but as what follows makes clear, this was not something I wanted to be true...

Later that night, I was talking to someone else on the team who had DID herself and I asked her if it had been obvious to her that I did, or if she'd seen any warning signs in me. Her response was 'Not really. Apart from when you talked about seeing a spider in your head [which I had] because one of my parts is a spider too...'

Now, I was still hugely phobic of spiders at that time – to the extent that I almost hadn't gone to Australia because I knew that it's full of them, and much bigger and more dangerous ones than we have in England. So, as the penny dropped that there was effectively a giant spider living in my head from which I could never escape, I completely freaked out. I started screaming hysterically saying, 'I can't live with that. I'm going to have to kill myself.'

Unsurprisingly, this alarmed the facilitator, who informed me that she was now obliged to contact the local mental health team. I begged her not to. I didn't want to be sectioned in Australia. And locked in a padded cell with only a giant spider for company! So I told her that I was confident I could get myself together and asked her to review the situation in the morning. Since it was already gone midnight, she reluctantly agreed. Thus began the strangest conversation of my life...

Having gone to my room, I said to the spider (who I understood was an 'alter' or dissociated part of myself, created by my brain to enable me to survive the literally unbearable horrors of my abuse but now having a mind and a will of its own), 'Okay, you're going to have to work with me here because I'm absolutely terrified of you and I want to run away but clearly we're stuck with each other so somehow we've got to find a way to coexist or we're both going to die and neither of us want that, right?! So, I accept that you're there and I'm willing to work with you but is there anything you can do to make yourself less terrifying...?'

Almost immediately, I heard the spider reply (a voice in my head), 'Well, everyone's scared of spiders but people seem to like ladybirds and really I'm just like a giant ladybird that's taken its red spotty jacket off... Does that help...?'

Well, yes, actually, it really did. And not just because of the wisdom of the words but because of the softness of the voice in which they were spoken...

Cut to the next morning and after a reasonable night's sleep (in the circumstances!) the spider and I were getting along famously. He (I think he's a he) had also explained that he was like a machine that I had created to terrify others and so protect myself, what clinicians call a 'protector part'. So he had encouraged me to 'climb inside him', as if into the cockpit of a crane, and, as a result, I no longer felt frightened but hugely empowered. I had acted this out by wrapping a blanket (which, by coincidence, was red with black spots!) around my shoulders like a cloak of power, and I felt both euphoric and indestructible. Which was a bit of a surprise for the facilitator who had nervously asked me at breakfast how I was feeling only to be told, 'Yeah, great. The spider and I have come to an arrangement and it's all cool...'

But things went a bit wrong half an hour later when another team member told me it was time for the group session. Immediately I heard the spider say that he didn't want to go. So I said, 'Well, I'm sorry but I both want and need to go', to which his reply was a quite menacing 'Are you going to make me...?'

Suddenly I was afraid again. The peace I had negotiated with the spider was fragile to say the least and I didn't want to risk angering him, to face his wrath or even just encounter him in his unveiled form, his dark aspect. So I went into a more supplicant, pleading mode and said, 'Look, I really want to go in so could you please consider coming with me…?'

The spider said, 'Okay. I'll tell you what I'll do: I'll come into the session with you if you bow down before me and worship me as God!!!'

Now, you have to understand that I had been a committed Christian for 20 years at this point and not worshipping anyone or anything other than God is a fairly key principle of the Christian religion! Indeed, it's dealt with in the first and second commandments, so this was more than just a big ask; it was an impossibility. As I explained to the spider, I would rather be burnt at the stake or thrown to the lions than do that… His amused reply was, 'That's fine. I didn't expect you to say "yes"! But now you know how I feel: you asked me to do something. I told you I didn't want to do it but you tried to persuade me anyway. So I asked you to do something I knew you wouldn't want to do, so now we're even, aren't we?'

Which was all very reasonable – although I'm aware how crazy this sounds: having a conversation with a giant spider in my head that was, in one sense, a separate entity but ultimately, part of my own brain. And I realized afterwards (or even at the time) that it was like playing chess with myself: I could never win because my 'opponent' could predict my every move…

But then I remembered what one of the facilitators had said at the beginning of the course: 'This is "inner child" work. And if you're lucky enough to establish contact with your inner child [or, in my case, inner children!] for goodness sake, do whatever they ask – however random or bizarre – because they're telling you what they need and if you don't do it, you may never hear from them again, or at least you'll drive them even further away…'

And suddenly I knew that underneath the sinister – even 'Satanic' – exterior, this was just a damaged part of me, testing me to see if I really meant it when I said that I loved and accepted it and was willing to work with it. So, on that understanding I said, 'Okay. Well, I hope you realize that this goes against everything I've believed and held most dear for

20 years but to show you that I'm serious about this...' And I got down on my knees and bowed before the spider – who I couldn't actually see other than in my mind's eye – something I would never have believed I would do even earlier that morning.

When I finished – and it only took a few seconds – the spider said, 'That's not good enough. I want your wholehearted worship...' Well, I nearly exploded and said, 'You're taking the mickey now! I would literally have died before doing that till five minutes ago but I did it for you, to show you how serious I am and now you want more?! Forget about it!' To which the spider's calm reply was, 'Okay. Well, you gave me half of what I asked for, so I'll do the same: I'll come into your stupid session but I'll talk all the way through it. You won't be able to concentrate. But if that's good enough for you...'

It was. And I could see that it wasn't reasonable to ask him to give me more than I'd been willing to give him so I went in – 'we' went in – and actually the spider didn't do what he'd threatened: he shut up or disappeared or went to sleep or whatever alters do. And I realized later that this was because I had given him enough: I'd shown him I was willing to go to any lengths for him which was what he needed, what I had needed (and never got) as a child. And there are two postscripts to this story.

One: the following day, when I left the course and got to my hotel room, I was overcome with gratitude to the spider for giving me 100 per cent of what I'd asked for when I hadn't done the same for him. So now I wanted to repay the favour. So I got down on my hands and knees in my hotel room and gave him the wholehearted worship I hadn't felt able to give him before. And instantly I felt him transform from a terrifying monster into a joyful child – albeit a still spidery one – and I/we literally danced for joy around the room...

Then (two) a few years later, after I'd done lots of therapy and help set up and run the same course in the UK a few times, we were doing an exercise in which we were asked to say what we had needed as a child and hadn't got. And as we went round the room and others said, 'To be loved, cherished, nurtured, protected, enjoyed' (all of which applied to me as well), the phrase that popped into my mind and felt like what I

> wanted to say, what I wished my parents had done for me, was 'I needed to be worshipped.' As I believe all babies should be. And I certainly did that for my children – in a non-first commandment-breaking way – and I'm glad that, by the grace of God, I was willing and able to do that for my friend the spider...

The conversation within

The voices within our minds can relate to us in many different ways. They can seem so other, so evil, that they must be demonic. They can seem so much something that I would not have thought, and yet so good, that they must be God. I can be sure that the thought was 'mine', or at least that it spoke for a part of me, and yet it might still seem to have a life of its own. This inner conversation can be not only psychologically complicated, but also spiritually and theologically complicated. What if the thoughts I have are blasphemous? Am I 'responsible'? Do I need to confess and repent the thoughts that I did not invite or welcome, and which I dearly wish would leave me? I am not wishing to present trite or simplistic answers here, and, in any case, we are all different. A search for anything approaching a satisfactory answer will probably lead to counselling, psychotherapy or spiritual direction. However, it is important to acknowledge the conversation.

Dominic's conversation with the spider was psychologically, spiritually and theologically complex. Initially, he was tempted to view this as a demonic intrusion, but recognizing that this was a conversation with something that needed to be owned as belonging to the self enabled it to be dealt with both more creatively and with a better eventual outcome.[9] The encounter raises significant theological challenges, to which Dominic responds with courage, faith, wisdom and prayer. The things that we find within ourselves are sometimes frightening, and often ambiguous. Faith provides a context within which we may confront them with assurance of divine protection. It creates a safe space within which to have the conversation.

---

9 Exorcism seems to be especially unhelpful for people identified as suffering from dissociative identity disorder (Fraser 1993).

Chapter 11

Evil Company

Christian scripture and history provide accounts of many evil voices, from the serpent in the Garden of Eden to the demons exorcised by Jesus, the devils of Loudun, contemporary accounts of 'deliverance ministry' and the apocalyptic Beast of Revelation. The historical, anthropological and psychological relationship between these voices and those of various psychiatric syndromes (notably, but not exclusively, schizophrenia) is complex.[1] On the one hand, scientifically reductive accounts seek to explain everything in cultural and/or psychiatric terms. At the other extreme, and very controversially, there are those who would explain schizophrenia in terms of demonology.[2] In between these extreme positions, there are more nuanced accounts.[3] These debates will not be further rehearsed here. However, it is important to acknowledge that some voices that Christians hear have what may best be described as evil content, and are the more distressing because of that. It is also important to recognize that the different views that Christians hold on such matters, combined with differences between scientific and religious perspectives, set the

1 See, for example, Cook (2018); Enoch and Ball (2001, pp.224–244); Kemp and Williams (1987); and Montgomery (1976).

2 Irmak (2014). See correspondence from Karanci (2014) and Scrutton (2015).

3 The Church of England, for example, requires that deliverance ministry should be undertaken in liaison with mental health services (Perry 1996), neither ascribing everything to mental disorder, nor ruling out the possibility of evil influence that in some way or another is not reducible to mental disorder.

scene for unhelpful misunderstandings. They mitigate against access to integrated, informed and effective clinical or pastoral care.

The two examples given in this chapter were both associated with a psychiatric diagnosis. Research shows that a major discriminating factor between voices that are associated with a psychiatric diagnosis and those that are not is that the former are more often distressing and associated with negative affect.[4] Like other voices, evil voices are usually associated with a sense of presence and agency. They are not just 'voices'. If companion voices (discussed in Chapter 7) may be understood as good friends, then the voices under consideration here are the opposite. They are a kind of companion, but with evil valence. We may say, without prejudice to any theological arguments about ontology, that they are a kind of evil company.

The author of the first story included here found her voices distressing to the extent that it was difficult to talk or write about them. She adopts a telegraphic style that is all the more evocative of the experience for not being translated into a grammatical narrative, and I have included it here exactly as she wrote it down for me.

PERPETUA'S STORY:[5] EXPERIENCES OF VOICE HEARING

During first year at Oxford, pretty miserable, lonely, not coping

My second year at Oxford things really began to unravel

Voices first happened in a church service

At first just one voice. I just knew it was the devil

'The devil is calling you'

'You cannot escape'

Petrified

Happened several occasions, same sort of thing

Asked priest for help

He told me I was possessed

Had exorcism – 4 spirits cast out

Had sort of fit and found myself on the floor

4 Davies, Griffin and Vice (2001); Johns *et al.* (2014); Peters *et al.* (2017).

5 Pseudonym.

So relieved afterwards – on a high for about a month
But this did not last
Heard the devil again about one week later
Again in a evangelical church service, saying similar sorts of things
'You are possessed'
'You cannot hide this'
'You are under control'
'I will make you dangerous'
'You will pay with your life'
Terrified

Struggling with work

Thought everyone knew that I was possessed

I had more prayer, but this did not work, and I found that going to church just made the devil very angry

He would say things like 'You've committed unforgivable sin', 'You'll be sent to hell'

I was still struggling with work.

Yet again I tried to re-commit myself to God. Someone else from the church prayed with me and I renounced the devil and told him he had no place in me.

Again it was better for a while

Then he came back, this time he brought his friends (see what happens if you sweep the place clean but leave it empty, Matthew 12). Then I had several voices, I called them the spirits. They talked about me a lot. Sometimes they would just describe what I was doing in very mocking tones, 'Oh she's walking down the street now', or 'What does she think she's doing?', etc., etc.

They also made very derogatory comments at times, which were crippling especially if I was trying to do something/work. They would tell me I couldn't do things, that they were in control, that I was upsetting people, that everybody knew everything about me.

I took to alcohol to numb things. That was my only way of keeping going.

Things just went from bad to worse.

Seemed to be lots of voices, they talked about what they would do with me, how they would keep me in hell, how they would never leave me, they would always control my thoughts. Quite often they would laugh and laugh about me and how they were going to torture me.

I had a curious form of hell, which was listening to the screams and cries of all the people I had hurt/damaged/destroyed so I would have to think about my guilt for eternity. This was devised by the spirits.

One day I saw some of these spirits who were coming in and out of me as dancing shadowy creatures on my bedroom wall. They told me to burn their shapes onto my arms and legs as a mark of my submission to them. I did this with matches and I still have the scars.

Eventually things came to crisis

My thoughts were controlled by them, I couldn't think straight at all.

The devil himself (which I recognize as louder, and more from outside me than the other spirits) told me that I was destroying the world. He said that unless I killed myself, they would kill my parents. I was in a kind of daze, and could not speak, could not put any words together. I was like that for many months.

It was at this point that I attempted suicide and was hospitalized for so long.

I am much better now.

When I am stressed, they come, and they can rapidly take over if I'm not careful.

There are various things which help.

Medication helps to an extent, but is only part of the answer.

I have various tactics:

Distraction is my favourite. I know they are devils, therefore they tell lies, therefore listening to them is the worst thing I can do, and is actually what they want me to do. So if I can possibly ignore them and get on with something else it helps. It helps to do creative things, like writing, playing music, reading articles etc., rather than watch TV or other passive occupations.

I know from experience that arguing with them is a recipe for disaster – they just get louder and angrier. So I avoid that. Sometimes I can tell them I'll speak to them later, but that does not always work.

I know that they have bad theology. I do not believe that there is such a thing as unforgivable sin. I do not really believe in the existence of hell. I do not think God wants to have me completely trapped in guilt. Also, I know that being devils, they are not as powerful as God, and this idea that they might give me all this power to destroy everything is not tenable. Also to think that I am that special, that this is happening only to me, is bad theology and totally unrealistic.

I always have the radio on at night, they can be bad then. I try not to get too stressed about anything. I try not to be too intense about religion or expose myself to evangelism, etc. I try to pray, and be mindful, living one day at a time and being thankful for it. I feel very fortunate to have such a full life and opportunities now, and I can hardly believe how things have changed for the better.

The second story included here relates a very different, and highly creative, way of coping that has proved very successful over a number of years.

CLARE'S[6] STORY: THE VOICE

When I was a child, about four to five years old, occasionally a small purple dragon-like monster would appear within my mind to help me with things/make conversation. I was quite aware that he was a figment of my imagination, as what he did was controllable and dictated by me and easily interrupted by my surroundings but I did enjoy talking to him and encouraged his presence when he was there. At 13 years old, I heard the Voice of that monster again, still within my mind but completely uninvited, speaking as if with a megaphone to snap me out of my afternoon reverie. His words were so obscene that I blocked them out, hoping that whatever this voice had been, it never came back. But I heard the Voice again two weeks later, then five days, then hourly until the bombardment of disturbing and distasteful words and phrases were pummelling my mind every few seconds. At the age of 15 it was infiltrating my dreams to wake me on mornings, whilst keeping me from sleeping for hours at night. My eyes were shadowed by dark rings and some nights I would be screaming aloud for it to stop. It was at this time that the Voice started saying that other people could read

6 Pseudonym.

my thoughts. My shame meant I hated leaving the house and could no longer look people in the eye. I went to see a doctor at this point and became a patient with Early Intervention in Psychosis (EIP), part of Child and Adolescent Mental Health Services. This help for people with mental illness under 18 years old gave me access to a psychiatrist, cognitive behavioural therapist [CBT] and two counsellors. I was spoilt for being able to talk about my problems but I couldn't tell any of them the offensive things that plagued me, as I was so ashamed and due to their apparent lack of personal religion and projected lack of awareness of spiritual issues, I often felt it was pointless to talk about the spiritual connections the Voice made towards my sexuality and sexual fears.

In an attempt to diminish the Voice my psychiatrist put me on aripiprazole but my hands would seize up after five minutes of writing. With no difference to the voice after one year we switched to olanzapine. This did diminish the voice but only by sedating me. Even on half of the lowest dose I would struggle to keep my eyes open and my body upright throughout the day, even after 10 hours of sleep and several coffees. The Voice still spoke of all of the same things that I couldn't bring myself to tell anyone but my psychiatrist wouldn't let me come off it until my exams were over. I couldn't wait this long. I needed my bouncy brain back to do my maths, so I took myself off it. My brain was buzzing and the Voice was worse than it had been in a very long time but there were no blocks in my mind, I could think and process maths again just in time to do my A-level exams. Although the Voice was worse, my CBT had taught me ways to cope (even if my therapist didn't know what I was coping with) and I was discharged from EIP. I then had a summer with absolutely nothing to do but relax. The Voice got a lot better, even off the medication. However, the olanzapine did teach me how to relax even more, simply because whilst on it I hadn't the energy to react to things the way I used to. Realizing that nothing particularly bad happened when I couldn't react, I was able to not be such a perfectionist. I had always been a high achiever and still do feel like life is, amongst other things, a journey to make you a better person. This foundational feeling within me means that I have constantly striven for perfection. A lot of life's lessons have been about teaching me that perfection doesn't exist and to just be the best that I can be. However, during my teenage years

I believed that perfection could be reached and so unless I was getting the top grades (in some things I would only settle for 100 per cent) I felt very guilty and a failure. The Voice would stem from this guilt but even more; it grew from the stress of having to achieve perfection in each new endeavour. It would talk about work and how inadequate I was in that regard but 90 per cent of what it said (and what it had said when I first heard it) was sexually orientated, to do with abuse towards me. Both would worsen in direct proportion to the amount of work I had to do. This still is something I need to watch, although my drive to perfection is significantly reduced now compared to then, olanzapine being a big turning point for this.

The summer that I was 17, in the space between switching between aripiprazole and olanzapine, I did some evangelizing around Newcastle City with a group of friends from church. This consisted of a group of people from a church in Norway joining with our church and together we split off into different groups to spread the Gospel on the streets of Newcastle. This involved having direct conversations with people, chatting to them about their issues, how God could help, giving them church fliers and praying with them. This experience turned out to be just as much about helping me as it was about helping others and I truly believe this was part of God's Divine Plan to set me back on my feet. During this week I became close to a Norwegian leader and a leader from my church and felt comfortable enough to tell them that I was hearing the Voice. I was even able to share some of the deepest and darkest things that it had been saying to me from the beginning. As I talked to them we prayed that God would release me from any guilt and enter my heart in place of where this guilt had been. I felt warm and peaceful like I hadn't in years. The Voice didn't talk for two days, although it was banging on the doors in the back of my head, attempting to break back in (originally the Voice had started at the front of my mind, then spread throughout my whole head, always being stronger at the front. After this spiritual experience I felt like it was pushing to come back in via the doors I presumed it had exited in the 'back of my head'). After two days I wasn't strong enough to hold up the barricades anymore and the entourage came bursting back through. However, this feeling of evil trying to break down the walls of my mind and the fact that it had gone away with prayer played on my ever-pressing ideas that I was possessed. To help put me at ease that I wasn't possessed, after much badgering, my parents agreed to call the church minister to perform an exorcism. After a very useful and calming conversation he said, 'I know you are not possessed but I will perform an exorcism anyway.' When the Voice continued to speak just as loudly afterwards I knew that I wasn't possessed and was able to let that idea go. This fear of possession illustrated just how deeply my illness was intertwined with my religion, and although I found prayer comforting, fearing power of the spiritual always made the Voice get louder and less easy to block when I prayed. It was in this summer of relaxation that my ideas of religion started turning, becoming beneficial to my healing rather than detrimental. I became bolder to tell people at church what was going on and although a few were not helpful (they also believed it was an Evil Spirit) many, particularly a doctor and psychiatrist, were very helpful by listening, praying with me and helping me find God.

Over the relaxing summer, I stopped believing so much that people could read my thoughts, mainly because I had been testing people: 'If you can read my mind, do (action).' No one ever did the 'actions' I proposed. So at this time I became very sociable, spending much of my time in the company of friends and family and rarely time alone. It was during this period that I realized how much I craved the company of people and how much social contact I had been missing during my studies, no doubt contributing to stress and my illness. When I went to university at the end of that summer I socialized with so many different groups of people and went on every night out that was advertised. I do not regret meeting and talking to anyone that I did in that time but the sleep deprivation, the drinking and homesickness started to close in on me and by week seven I was very ill again, the Voice talking loudly at me, sometimes multiplying to not just the sole male voice but into more men and even a few women, who would all gather round and babble at my head, giving me no space to think between them. It was at this point, when I was afraid I would snap and expose the Voice to all of these new friends, that I decided to do what I knew I should but had been postponing for so long. I had to stop blocking the Voice out and listen to what it was trying to tell me. So it was towards the end of that seventh week that I took myself away to my bedroom and double-locked my door. I was afraid that if the Voice overwhelmed me and I lost control of myself that my housemates would see me in such a state. So I lay on my bed and prayed that God would hold onto me and keep me safe, no matter what the Voice said or where it tried to take me. Then I let go.

I instinctively knew that the Voice only talked so much because I entertained it. The Voice talking at me consisted of: 'If you don't do (OCD[7] behaviour), then (something horrific/obscene) will happen to (myself/a named person, usually a family member) and (so it will be your fault)', or '(something horrific/obscene) has happened (to myself/named person) because you didn't do (OCD behaviour)', so I would always just perform the OCD behaviour, in an attempt to block the Voice out and keep it at bay. But one bout of OCD behaviour was never enough, so I would repeat it and embellish it with added OCD behaviours (as I was told to) until I was stuck in a cycle. The Voice would say, 'Now you have done (OCD behaviour) but not well enough and if you don't do (another OCD behaviour) to cancel out the one you didn't do well enough (something horrific) will still happen and if (something else horrific) happens as well it'll be your fault.' And so it would escalate like this.

Examples of some of the OCD behaviours consisted of saying 'cancel' in my head (according to the Voice this was to cancel from the other the obscene thing it had said was going to happen). Although the Voice originally said that just saying 'cancel' was enough, immediately afterwards it would say that it wasn't because I was sitting in a certain way (often it was because I was sitting with my feet on the ground – if I cancelled anything I would be obliged to lift them, invisibly to everyone else, off the ground – or my hands, knees or elbows were touching any object). The Voice said that because I had voided my 'cancelling' in this way I would have to repeat the process but with twice as much power (meaning that I would have to say 'cancel' in my head, twice). At the same time I would have to tap for a specified amount of time the place that I had been touching, with the same body part that had 'voided' it the first time. If the timing of the tap was out of time with the

---

7 OCD stands for obsessive compulsive disorder. The term is used here by Clare herself, and is not the diagnosis made by her psychiatrist.

'cancelling' or wasn't long enough, I would have to do it again but twice as hard as the last time (now say 'cancel' four times). The cancelling grew like this in an exponential way and whether I was told by the Voice to perform these behaviours was unaffected by whether I was having conversations with people or not.

The strain on me to perform these 'OCD behaviours' correctly whilst maintaining focus and input to conversations was often very great. Once I was in this 'cancelling' cycle it became more and more difficult to maintain it, particularly to remember how many 'cancels' I had done, and it would end with me forgetting where I was, having to do a few taps with my hands/feet on whatever object was nearest (it always had to be an even number), and then an internal mental argument with the Voice as to how what I had done was enough. Then that would end and within a few seconds the Voice would start again. If I went against the Voice and refused to perform the OCD behaviours, I would get more and more distressed until I just did as it said, providing a small amount of relief until it came back with vengeance the next time. There were also some words that I was forbidden to say: 'rather', 'yes', 'deal' and 'swear' were amongst the most forbidden, words that suggested finality. Blasphemy was completely forbidden and even pained me to hear other people say it. Blasphemy still makes me feel uncomfortable and still sets the Voice off sometimes. My fear of words representing finality also had a spiritual connection, and this fear started at about the same time that I developed fears that I was possessed but lasted beyond when fears of possession subsided. The Voice said that if I was to say any of these words, or other words suggesting finality, that that would mean I was agreeing to sell my soul to the Devil and that I would no longer have control over my body; the Devil would, and I wouldn't remember any of the awful things that the Voice would say it would make my body do. Those words represented the finality/end of my eternal life, as my soul would be taken by the Devil. This was one of the things that it kept me awake at night with – the fear that I would lose control of my body and murder my family in my sleep! However, these 'words of finality' were only directed towards me for the first few months that it started saying it, then they became directed at other people, so if I was to say a 'word of finality' whilst looking at someone/even to think one of the listed words I would have to do the 'cancelling' process but would still be fearful that if that person did turn out to do something bad (this could involve just talking unkindly) this would show that their body had been overtaken by an evil spirit and they were going to do evil things in the future, particularly sexual things like rape, and it was all my fault.

So it was in my room at university that I decided to completely 'let go' and didn't try and block or relieve it with any OCD behaviours. To do this I had to put my trust in something bigger than It and myself.

At first the Voice shouted at me and did that thing that it had started doing recently, multiplying into several different voices. Then, as the words washed over me, I started listening to them, until they led me back through memories until the first time it had spoken, then I started going back even further, highlighting insecurities and experiences that I was conflicted with and were triggering the Voice to start talking. Throughout this experience I cried incessantly, then the Voice started to peter off and became silent. No daemons were banging on any doors in the back of my head; nothing was there to knock. I lay still in the darkness of my room, only the thickness of a heavy silence ringing in my ears. At this I cried all over again and thanked God unremittingly for such peace and for holding onto me throughout. Then I slept like I hadn't slept in years. This peace lasted for two days, until the Voice started trickling back in. But I just repeated the process, now a lot shorter and more easily solved than the first time, with a lot less tears. Within a week after the main cleansing experience I found an amazing church, full of people who supported me when I told them about the Voice and that I was now a lot more equipped to help if any of them were struggling mentally. Just like with the evangelizing, helping others turned out to be extremely beneficial to healing myself.

When I had found more spiritual clarity other things in my life that I needed to change became clear: quitting caffeine (turned down the activity in my brain significantly) and sugar and took up running, daily. I also started forcing myself to do any impending tasks that I had, where I could, as soon as I got them, so that they wouldn't be hanging over me and start stressing me out. I also made an effort to surround myself with activities that would keep my brain occupied and people that were good for me and brought me up, so that I had the strength to help those who were possibly feeling weak without coming down myself. Those life decisions were made three to four years ago but even now, a month away from turning 22 years of age, I am adding to the list. About a year ago I quit drinking, even though I was only doing it about once monthly, because it wasn't worth the effect on my mood and mind. I have also started praying, meditating and reading spiritual passages from the Bible and other love-filled passages that resonate with me and help me develop. To give the coming day to God/Source of Everything works on the same principle as 'letting go' did when I was 18 in my room at university. To accept that I am out of control and God is in control is a skill that I will admit I do not yet completely have, but every major experience like this brings me closer to him and helps me let go a little bit more.

My body is extremely sensitive to the environment and I believe that I am quite sensitive to the spiritual and I wouldn't change these sensitivities for anything. That I become mentally unwell when I am even slightly unbalanced is a blessing because it protects me from harm. That my senses are heightened means the beautiful things in life are spectacular. For me, to accept my body, all aspects of my personality and my insecurities and work with them has made me not only feel peace, but like I have found that niche that God created for me to fill. He certainly did 'Knit me together in my mother's womb' (Psalm 139.13). I would encourage everyone, whether mentally ill or not, to embrace those facets of personality that may cause feelings of discomfort and speak to them directly, to ask why they think the way they do because it will open doors to your inner being that may well lead to healing, peace and a connection to God/Source that you were previously unaware was there.

Evil company

Perpetua and Clare have in common a Christian faith which, in most respects, provided the basis for a resilient and effective coping response to a very distressing experience. However, that same faith provides a framing within which evil can seem to be a very real threat. Notwithstanding an Augustinian tradition which denies that evil has any ontological substance, contemporary charismatic, Pentecostal and Catholic traditions all acknowledge at some level that there is sometimes a pastoral need for 'deliverance' or exorcism, a prayerful recourse to divine authority over evil powers. Exorcism narratives are a central feature of the Synoptic Gospel accounts of Jesus's Galilean ministry, and attempts to demythologize them have never been popular in churches that take a more literal approach to the interpretation of biblical texts.

Whatever one makes of the Gospel accounts, and whatever theology or experience one might put forward in favour of retaining some kind of ritual of deliverance or exorcism within the ambit of the churches' ministry, exorcism is sometimes deeply unhelpful. In particular, it generally seems to be found harmful where a diagnosis of dissociative identity disorder has been made.[8] Nor does it seem to be effective for many other psychiatric disorders.[9] Similarly, in both of the present stories, exorcism was largely ineffective although it did produce some temporary relief and, in Clare's case, a reassurance that she was not possessed.

In both of the narratives presented here, psychiatric treatments proved only partly effective. Both Perpetua and Clare have learned their own ways of dealing with their voices. For both of them, notwithstanding initially unhelpful and naïve attempts to find a simple solution through prayer, prayer has eventually played an important part in recovery. This has come about both through prayer with others – where those others have been wise and discerning in the kind of prayer they have offered – and through Perpetua and Clare each finding their own approach to establishing a prayerful routine of life.

Discussions about ontology and demonology may be theologically interesting, but they do not seem to be clinically or pastorally helpful when seeking to help people who hear 'demonic' voices. There can be few other clinical or pastoral issues that are so controversial or prone to

8 See Chapter 10. See also Bowman (1991) and Fraser (1993).

9 Pfeifer (1994).

misunderstanding between mental health professionals and members of Christian communities, and yet so much in need of a collaborative approach to providing care.[10]

10 Similar considerations apply in relation to Islamic communities (see Blom and Hoffer 2012; Dein and Illaiee 2013).

Chapter 12

Complex Company

I have devoted this chapter to one story that deserves to be heard in full. It brings together themes from many, if not all, of the previous chapters, and sets them in the context of Christian life. It is a story about finding faith, and about an emerging awareness of the complex company kept by inner voices. It is a story about learning to pray. It is a story about recovery and grace.

RACHEL'S STORY: VOICE HEARING AND CHRISTIANITY

> Hi Jesus, it's Rachel here. I'm just writing to you because I can't say it in my head without the shouting and voices so I am scared to pray to you but Satan wants me not to but screw him, but to get around this I am writing to you instead.

This diary entry illustrates my confusion around Christianity and voice hearing. Through my journey of recovery from anorexia and depression, the complicated relationship between spirituality and psychiatry has been very personally and often painfully lived through. I believe God speaks to us, and we can listen for him, and talk back. I also have a voice that speaks to me, that I listen for, and talk back to. Are both real? Or are both figures of my imagination? Can I talk to one without the other hearing?

Or do I have to choose? Am I reducing God to just a voice, or elevating the voice to a god?

These are some of the questions my mental illness and my faith have led me to grapple with over the past few years. Mental illness affects all parts of a person's life, including their spirituality. Professionals can have stigma about religion, and religion can have stigma about mental health. As a Christian whose mental health became tangled up in faith, I found myself feeling quite lost and alone somewhere between the two, unsure if it was an issue for doctors or pastors. Over time, with the help of professionals, Christian friends, and a lot of prayer and thinking, I am making some kind of sense of what for me became a knotted mess. This process has been fundamental to my recovery, and has strengthened and deepened my faith profoundly – in fact, I feel privileged to have been on this (at times quite dark) journey because of all I've learned through it.

I'm going to tell my story, and explain how I have come to make sense of the complex and profound relationship been voice hearing and Christianity. I stress that the ideas and issues are a snapshot of my personal thoughts in the middle of a process rather than a conclusion, and will quite possibly keep changing along the journey I'm on.

I had what can only be described as an idyllic childhood, as I saw it. As one of four children, the house was always busy and our days were always busier with games, dens and countryside walks. I developed a strong sense of identity as part of my family. From a young age being a Christian has been a part of my life. Before I was old enough to decide this myself, this took the form of outings and playing with people from church – my parents ran the youth club and a music group, and so church was a big part of family life. We'd go on trips with the youth group, and some people would come to babysit or play with us. One of these people who came around to play sexually abused me. At the age of seven I liked the attention – having time alone with a much older boy who wanted to play with just me made me feel special. From my perspective, everything was great.

My early teenage years were a mixed experience, with one foot in the family I was so closely knitted to, and the other with new friendships and the independence I was forming as I grew up and tried to carve my own identity. I set my sights on being the best I could at everything I did, partly because I enjoyed new challenges, but in retrospect, probably also to boost my self-esteem that had been wobbled by bullying. On top of this, puberty brought additional stresses. As I started to develop an understanding of sex and relationships from patchy sex education lessons by awkward teachers and schoolyard rumours, I began to think that perhaps the games I played with the older boy from church weren't just games. As my body changed, I began to realize that the butterflies that I felt with people I had young teenage crushes on felt the same as the feelings I got when I habitually replayed through what had happened when I was seven in my mind. Something didn't seem quite right about it, but I didn't understand what or why. I realized I had a secret, and one that was different to the kind my friends told me on slow ambles home from school. My family didn't seem to keep big secrets from each other – we respected everyone's personal lives whilst trusting each other to share important things. But I had a confusing secret that didn't feel like something I should share. This made me feel powerful – it was mine – but also a little distanced from my family; I didn't understand why, but I knew I was keeping something big from them which I didn't think was the right thing to do. This gave me a bad feeling inside.

During this period, my faith became my own. It was no longer just a lifestyle but my firm belief. This was aided by what I discovered for myself in the youth work at the new church my family had joined. I read the Bible and prayed by myself every morning, which whilst at the time was just a habit, I now realize was laying the foundations of trust in God's faithfulness for later years. Despite this, I lacked any real understanding of God's grace for us. I was trying to be good to earn God's favour, I didn't understand it was a gift I was freely given. Thus, my secret that gave me a bad feeling didn't seem like something I could pray about, so I kept it tightly away in a box, out of reach of the box I tried to put God in. I was encouraged to listen for God speaking to me, that he is a personal God and wants a close relationship with us, and so will speak to us. I started to listen to God speaking to me through the Bible, other people, and through pictures and words he gave to me in the quiet space in my mind. As I listened to the voice of God, I learned that I had a very intimate relationship with him. Needless to say that later, when I developed a very intimate relationship with another voice I sometimes heard in my mind in that same quiet space, I was confused and distressed.

By the age of 16 as life pressures of friends, futures and wanting to do well in exams were pressing down hard on me, the past began to bubble up. The increasing awareness of my own sexuality, coupled with the emergences of many high-profile child abuse cases, made me begin to realize that what happened to me as a child was bad. Yet I had kept it inside of me, I hid it from my friends, family and from God. It had become a part of me. If it was bad, so was I.

General anxiety of school and teenage life spiralled into depression. It was at this time I started to hear a voice. It was like my usual self-critical thoughts about, for example, not being good enough, fearing others didn't like me, or being too boring or lazy were being spoken in [an] unfamiliar way. It was always inside my head, but rather than being in the space that I did my own thinking and talked to myself in, it came from another place, the place where I listened to what other people were saying out loud to me. Over time it got increasingly removed from my own thoughts until it sounded like a male voice was speaking to me through earphones. It was quiet and manageable at first, generally saying things that weren't too removed from my own anxious thoughts, but because it was as if someone else was speaking them to me I believed them more. It would tell me I'd done things wrong, or that people were talking about me behind my back, that I'd done things that were upsetting and hurting others and that no one would believe me or care if I tried to talk about how I was feeling. It then started speaking to me about what I was beginning to understand as abuse, and I would listen and answer back. It would sometimes be accompanied by images of the abuse so I came to associate the voice I was hearing with the abuser. At this point I talked to no one but the voice about what had happened and how I felt about it. This only strengthened the voice, and isolated me further.

Over these months my mental health deteriorated and I fell into the grip of an eating disorder. I'd always tried to be 'good', the best I could be, and so from preteens I tried to be healthy. But, as I began to see myself more and more as a 'bad' person for what I kept inside of me, I tried to use eating to be 'good'. I became increasingly restrictive in my diet and compulsive about exercise. I also came to hate anything to do with sex, as to me it equated to abuse and the growing bad feeling inside of me. Thus, because we live in a world where the female body in particular is incredibly sexualized, I began to hate my body. I wanted to reverse the womanly developments of puberty that made boys try to put sticky hands on me at parties and say crude comments to me at school, and all the thoughts and feelings that came with it. To me, my body represented everything that was bad about me, and so I wanted to destroy it.

As this continued my mood fell further. I spent nights lying awake listening to the voice explain in seemingly perfect logic why I needed to destroy myself and how I was going to do it. I started to write things down to get it out of my head, and then when I couldn't find the words I started to draw it. I then lost the motivation for even this as I began to believe the voice. At my lowest, I was convinced that I had to kill myself, and that if I didn't, the voice would get other people to do it for me. I thought that it was what was best for me, my family, and what God must want.

I eventually did ask for help, primarily with eating, but as I told people snippets of what was going on in my head I was passed from one mental health team to another; by the time I got to the first assessment with one, I was too unwell and had to be referred on to another team. I started to lose hope that things could ever get better.

It was at this point that I first disclosed the abuse to a church youth leader. I started to have flashbacks and nightmares about what had happened, and whilst I didn't understand how, I decided that it probably was a contributing factor to my deteriorating mental health. I was shocked and scared by how seriously everyone took it. Why was everyone else reacting in such a different way to me? What I thought was just a silly secret had resulted in the police knocking on my door for interviews and asking me to make decisions about things I couldn't understand. Something that I thought was very personal and secret, something that made me special, was being brashly handed from one stranger to another. The most private and ugly part of me was given to [the] police, doctors, nurses, teachers, friends and family. Everyone knew I'd been keeping a secret I shouldn't have been. I was embarrassed, distressed and confused, so retreated further towards the only two voices that I felt understood me – the voice of God and the voice in my head.

With all this going on as I approached my final A-levels, I went from being a healthy weight in January to being rushed into the high monitoring ward of the assessment suite in casualty in May. Wires and tubes were shoved into and stuck onto me. I didn't understand what was happening, I didn't think I was this ill. A chaplain came to give the last rights to the elderly lady in the bed next to me. That night, as my parents left me in the dark ward surrounded by rushed doctors and nurses and the flashing and beeping of machines, I realized I was both physically and mentally touching death. I had very nearly completely destroyed myself.

Where was God at this time? I realize now, he was carrying me.

In the months leading up to this night, I felt alone in my head with just God and the voice for company. I couldn't even begin to explain what was going on to my family or friends as they desperately tried to support me with tireless patience. I just didn't understand what was happening. But God and the voice seemed to understand, and God, and also the voice, could soothe me. Yet these relationships were causing me distress. I talked with both in the same place in my head – how did I know who was who? If the voice was just my mind playing tricks on me, as doctors told me, was God also? But I firmly believed God is real, and thus so must the voice be. The doctors were all wrong and I needed to stop talking to them. Whenever I tried to clear my mind to pray, the voice would start talking. It would tell me I was praying to it instead of God, and that I worshipped it, which was making God very angry with me. It would tell me God couldn't hear my prayers as it had intercepted them, and only allowed certain bits through, and so I had to say prayers over and over again in the hope one would slip through and get to him.

Up until this point, God was my rock. Spending time with him was the only thing that kept me going because he gave me hope. I would meditate on scriptures and pour out my heart through tears, sometimes getting angry about why I felt he'd forsaken me, and sometimes thanking him for his comfort. I could challenge suicidal thoughts because I knew that if God had created me, it must be for a reason, and so I must have some worth to him, and some role to play here on earth. But, as the voice got louder, I became too frightened to pray as this meant I had to listen to the voice too, and it would get angry with me. I was scared about what it might make me do. This was incredibly isolating. It made me feel alone in the storm inside my head with just a destructive voice for company. I couldn't do it any longer. For me, an eating disorder was an SOS call, as I expressed with my body what I couldn't express in words. As horrendous as eating disorders are, it was a survival method and a lifeline that worked.

Once I was stable enough to leave the medical ward and be admitted to a specialist eating disorder inpatient unit, everything changed. I was so blessed by the care and support I received from the staff, other patients, my friends and family. As I started to realize that other people understood what I was battling, I slowly stopped confiding in the voice alone and shared my thoughts and feelings with other people, and the voice lost its power. Everyone seemed to understand and accept me in a way that I never thought could happen. I started to see hope. I was so determined to get my life back that I threw myself into recovery.

Every morning before the ordeal of the day, I'd have some quiet time with God, even though I was scared of what the voice would say as a result. If God could stick with me, I could stick with him. If praying in my head was too much, I'd whisper it out loud so I knew I wasn't accidentally speaking to the voice. If that didn't help, I'd write to God instead, and finally, if this was still too distressing, I'd lie on my bed hugging my knees and listening to worship music, and just be still knowing that God was there.

One night I remember clearly. I'd been sewing in the lounge that evening. When I got up to go to bed, a nurse followed me to my room and checked the fabric I had been sewing to make sure I wasn't hiding any embroidery needles in it that I could use to hurt myself. I wheeled over the feed I was attached to, that artificially gave my body the nutrients I refused to, and sat on my bed alone in the dark. The gravitas of the situation hit me. I was 18 years old, I'd had to drop out of school. I had to be away from my home, friends and family. I couldn't feed myself. I was so physically unstable I couldn't stand in the shower without the risk of blacking out; I was so mentally unstable that I couldn't be trusted with a blunt needle. Academic excellence, sporting and musical achievements, friends, family, church, future plans, all of the things I had once built my life on had been taken away. I was nothing. I remembered a Bible verse from Hosea 2.14 that had spoken to me a few months before – 'I am now going to allure her; I will lead her into the wilderness and speak tenderly to her' – and I understood what it meant in that moment. I looked up and saw my whiteboard that I'd written comforting Bible verses on: 'child of God', 'free from condemnation', 'saved by grace', 'comforted by God in troubles', 'sustained by God', 'carried by God', 'inseparable from God', 'soaring on wings like eagles', 'delighted in', 'given a hope and a future', 'loved', 'God's masterpiece', 'redeemed', 'holy and blameless in his sight', 'carried by God'. If God thought all these things about me even in the state I was in, after I'd fallen so far, when I had nothing to offer him but the empty shell of a person I'd become, then he must always think them, I must always be this loved. This was when I found God's grace. I realized I had what I didn't deserve, a life, a hope, a future that I couldn't earn. I couldn't be separated from God's love. God knew about my past and my fears and failures, he heard every conversation I'd had with the voice. This was the turning point in me starting to realize that nothing at all, no voice or evil, was closer or understood me more than God did. It was this firm foundation of unconditional love that I began to rebuild my life on.

I never really spoke to anyone about the voice as an inpatient. After the crisis team had told me I wasn't psychotic and told me it was tricks in my mind, I thought it must be irrelevant to my recovery. I felt silly, that everyone thought I was pretending, so kept it to myself after that. More significantly, it seemed to me like more of a spiritual concern than a psychiatric one, so it didn't seem appropriate to talk about. After a nurse saw me reading my Bible, I was told a chaplain could see me if I wanted to, but at the time I didn't realize it would be a mental health specialist and so thought they wouldn't understand, and I couldn't face trying to explain myself to another stranger. The only person I spoke to about the interaction between my mental health and my faith was my youth leader at church who happened to be a clinical psychologist. She was a real blessing as she understood both elements. She didn't dismiss my faith as just a hobby, as some mental health professionals did, and she didn't just tell me to pray about it or to have more faith, as some Christians did. If I hadn't by chance, or rather by God's perfect timing, had her in my life, I would have struggled to start to look past the distress to try to understand the complex interaction between my faith and mental health that was fundamental to recovering.

I made a very strong recovery from anorexia, fairly quickly. After five months as an inpatient I was a different person. It was like I hadn't recovered, but rather, I'd recovered the me that had been hidden under years of locking the distress and trauma inside of me. My relationships with friends and family were stronger than ever, I had started a new school year to finish my A-levels and was making new friends – my future looked brighter than ever. There were undoubtedly ups and downs, darker days and better ones, but it became clear I had learned to manage my mental health and live a full life without the destructive coping mechanism of an eating disorder.

A year later, whilst I was physically at peak health, and from the outside my life seemed sorted, the voice became louder and more intrusive. Everyday life became heavier and scarier. Whilst I had spoken through the abuse with my therapist in hospital, I realized I was yet to really process it. Flashbacks and nightmares returned, and my distress at my body grew. Prayer became an increasing struggle, and I began to feel alone with the voice again. Determined not to fall back into old self-destructive coping strategies, I realized that in order to make a sustainable recovery, I had to confront it head on, whether I wanted to or not.

For the first time, I was really serious about wanting the voice and difficult thoughts to change. My treatment team referred me to the psychology department that facilitated the process of change that I was finally ready to engage in. I was more open about my thoughts, feelings and the voice than I have ever been. Through this challenging process, I realized that the voice I heard sounded like the voice of the person who had abused me as a child. In my diary at this time I'd written, 'for some reason I think that the person who abused me is speaking to me through Satan, and thus I am talking to Satan, and so I am evil and can't talk to God and God doesn't hear me. I'm just a bit confused by it all'. Looking back, this was an understatement – I felt in despair.

I believed that I belonged to the voice. I had given hours and hours to listening to what I thought was the abuser talking to me. But the more I spoke about what had happened and came to understand that it was abuse, the more concerning this interaction with the voice became. At times I thought our minds were connected and so we were like the same person and shared thoughts, and so I was a danger to children too. This was incredibly distressing.

As well as this, because I thought Satan was liaising between me and the person who abused me, I thought it must be a Satanic voice. Was I possessed? Had I accidentally become a Satan worshipper? If so, did this put me out of the reach of God's love? This, coupled with the distress that came with processing the past and the fact that I was finding it very difficult to pray, made me think I must be evil. Some nights, the only way I could get to sleep was repeating Bible verses like 'nothing can separate me from the love of God' over and over again. I didn't fully believe it or accept it, but I knew it was true and so clung onto it.

I also started to think more about the things the voice said to me. As I worked through how the abuse had affected my view of sexuality, I realized the voice spoke about this a lot. It told me I was not pure, I was worthless, a slut because I could have stopped the abuse if I had wanted to, because at the time I enjoyed the attention, because I chose to think about what had happened so much. I wasn't 'fleeing from sexual immorality', as the Bible said to do; I was perpetually committing it by talking to the voice. I would ask for forgiveness over and over again. The voice and my disordered thoughts distorted what other Christians had taught me, some of which, on reflection, I disagree with. I'd been told that to be sexually intimate with someone is to give a part of yourself away, and so it irreversibly changes you. I thought I had already given my body to someone else, so it no longer belonged to me but the person who had abused me. Some Christian talks I'd heard about relationships spoke about the need for women to be 'helpful' to men who are more driven to be physical than women, and so the importance of not 'leading others on'. This fed the guilt I already felt, as I came to think I had encouraged the abuse, that it was my fault. The voice told me I was disgusting and sinful for trying to separate my sexuality from abuse and to think about the possibility of ever having a relationship. The hardest thing about it was that the voice could back up each argument with Bible verses, which, to my distorted mind, made complete sense, and so the voice was legitimized.

The voice also perpetuated my shame. It would tell me it was my fault. There was something wrong with me for not realizing it was abuse. Because I hadn't reported it to the police until years later, I was responsible for the abuser hurting other children. I knew Jesus died to end all my shame, but I found it hard to really believe it with this periodic reinforcement in my head, and harder to pray about it without the voice challenging me. But regardless of what I felt, I knew I needed God.

With a combination of therapy, and talking and praying about it with other Christians, I've started to untangle the voice and my faith, and on the whole find a peace about it. Sharing it with other Christians in the student group I was in was really powerful for me – no one else seemed to think there was something evil about me, even when I shared things about my past with them, which reassured me. They helped me to see the voice as just an artificial roadblock to God; from my side, it seemed huge and at times insurmountable, but from God's side, it had already been destroyed. I could view it as any other thing we can slip into thinking [that] gets in the way with our relationship with God like past hurts or sin, but that doesn't actually change the way God sees us. If these things don't stop God's love or might, neither could the voice.

In psychology sessions, I learned to think of the voice like any other relationship – sometimes positive, sometimes negative – but that didn't change who I was as a person. It's not right for anyone to say hurtful things to us, and if they do, it's not our fault. The voice was no different. No relationship with anyone else could cut me off from God, and neither could this one. With this mindset I was able to start to rationally explore what the Bible said on these issues for myself. I realized that if my worst-case scenario was true and that Satan was talking to me, I saw that Jesus had undeniably defeated all evil. If evil has no power over Jesus, and Jesus lives inside of me, evil has no power over me. I also tried to explore what the Bible said on sexuality. I was starting to accept that the abuse was in no way my fault and I had in no way sinned. But on hard days when I couldn't quite believe this, I realized that if my worst-case scenario was true and I had done something wrong, I could find no evidence that this could in anyway keep me from God. This really began to sink in as I read the story in the Bible of Jesus speaking to the woman who had committed adultery.

In response to being asked by Jesus who condemned her, the woman looked around, and saw no one did. Jesus then looked at her and said, 'Then neither do I.' If Jesus could sit down in the sand and speak to a woman who was morally, socially and physically rejected, about to be stoned to death for her sins, and say she was blameless in his eyes, by his grace, he could do the same for me.

No matter what I feel, I've come to realize that the voice in my head can in no way ever separate me from God, and if I start to forget this, I now know how to challenge it. Working through the trauma has really quietened the voice; it is, on the whole, small and weak, and I'm in control. But with life's stresses it does sometimes return and spark up the same old arguments. I can still lie in bed awake at night scared as I listen to its taunts, or daydream my way through conversations with people being preoccupied in my head before I have the chance to remind myself what is and isn't true. I still don't understand what it is, why I hear it, or if it will go away. But I've learned that whilst it is a part of my experience of life, it in no way changes who I am as a person. Regardless of my feelings or thoughts, I can remind myself that it has no power over me.

I count myself as blessed for the journey I've been on. I've seen the depth of God's grace, strength, patience, faithfulness and compassion in ways I would never have otherwise glimpsed. I've learned what it means to truly trust in God. I've learned more about my own strengths, vulnerabilities, values and passions. Finally, going close to death and choosing to fight for life means that every day is something I have chosen to live for, something I've had to really want, and so I've learned to appreciate life so much more than I could before.

I believe God's heart breaks even more than ours do over our sufferings and hurts. A wrong was done to me that has caused me a great deal of pain, and continues to negatively affect my life. God is as appalled by injustice as I am; as Isaiah 63.9 says, 'in all their distress he too was distressed'. Needless to say for a long time, and sometimes still, I long to undo my past and erase these hurts that should never have happened. Despite this, I accept my past. Whilst I am not defined by my trauma, voice or illness, I am defined by the fight I've fought to work through these things, and by the God I've found in the process.

> Had I not been on this journey, I wouldn't be the person I am today, and couldn't use my experiences to encourage others and share my insight. Because of this, I can accept with a peace that what happened can't be changed; my views and values about myself, my mental health and my faith, and life as a whole have been challenged and altered for good. That is something I don't want to change – I'm pleased to be me. I don't think everything happens for a reason, but I do believe that once it has happened, God makes all things work together for our good.

Complex company

Rachel likens the first emergence of the voice that she would later identify as that of her abuser with her own 'usual self-critical thoughts'. As that voice increasingly differentiated itself from her own thoughts, it became, in turn, the voice of her abuser and also something Satanic, setting itself (and trying to set Rachel) apart from God. Deeply critical, entangling itself with Rachel's own emerging adolescent awareness of her sexuality, it had the power to evoke shame. However, it also occupied the same inner space as God; it shared a similar intimacy of relationship. This voice and the voice of God became the only two voices that Rachel felt understood her. It could be a soothing voice; it could quote scripture. The complex inner company that Rachel found herself keeping became an entangled web of her own thoughts and two voices – the voice of God and 'the voice'.

The way out of this complex web was found with help from loving family and friends, as well as from mental health professionals. Not talking to others seemed to give the voice strength. This is only half the story, however, for Rachel's recovery is – I think – primarily a story about her relationship with God. As she found ways to pray despite the voice, her faith grew. As the things that she had held important were stripped away, she found that God was with her in the wilderness. From this point, she found grace to rebuild her life.

The lack of understanding of health professionals about Rachel's faith, and the lack of understanding of some Christians about what would be helpful in relation to mental health, threatened at times to reinforce Rachel's sense of isolation and guilt. A combination of therapy, talking and prayer helped to untangle the complex web. An awareness that a relationship with a voice is just that – a relationship, and not just a voice – provided another important stepping stone for Rachel's recovery. Ultimately, however, it was Rachel's relationship with God that brought about change, and it was her ability to engage theologically with her abuse, her voices and her isolation that enabled this relationship to grow.

Chapter 13

Christian Discernment

There are countless examples of visions and voices in Christian scripture and tradition, and the stories collected together in this book are in continuity with that inheritance. Abraham, Moses, Ezekiel, Jesus, Paul, Francis of Assisi, Julian of Norwich and Teresa of Calcutta, amongst many others, are all recorded as having heard a heavenly voice. Collectively, there would appear to be a large weight of testimony to support the contention that the voice of God may be heard by men and women.[1] Of course, these experiences are not necessarily all the same. We should not jump to the conclusion that the voices heard by Ezekiel, Jesus and Paul were all similar to each other in form, let alone that they were similar to those heard by Julian of Norwich or Teresa of Calcutta. There is scope for understanding a variety of forms that voices might take. For most of these voices, especially those in the Bible and in other historic texts, we know very little about exactly what form the voice did take. Were they the same as contemporary experiences, such as those reported in this book, or were they different? It is probably fair to say that they appear to have been the same in some ways, but different in others. However, we cannot really say for sure. We simply don't have enough information.

1 For a more detailed account of voices in scripture and Christian tradition, see Cook (2018).

It is also important to acknowledge that ancient texts and contemporary experiences all need to be interpreted. The biblical hermeneutical issues are well known. Not everyone agrees that Abraham or Moses were historical figures and, even if they were, we have no way of knowing exactly what their experiences were. The texts that we have are narratives, and the significance of the divine voice within a narrative is not necessarily to be equated with historical or psychological accounts of what may actually have happened. Similarly, the accounts of contemporary experiences included in the present book provide their own testimony to the interpretations that their authors place on what they heard. That does not mean that every reader will uncritically agree with them. Whilst I hope that readers will share my sense of respect for the integrity of what has generously been shared, and will appreciate the willingness of contributors to be vulnerable in so sharing their experiences, readers may still wish to form their own view about how such experiences have been shaped by culture, biography, community or faith. We know what these voices meant to those who heard them, but what might they mean for the rest of us?

The voice of caution

Alongside the tradition of visions and voices as revelatory of God, there is also a long tradition of caution about such experiences. In *The Literal Meaning of Genesis*, Augustine of Hippo (354–430 CE) distinguishes between corporeal, spiritual and intellectual visions. Corporeal visions are seen with the eye, spiritual visions with the mind, and intellectual visions – the highest form – are understood as completely without images. The more 'vision'-like the experience was, the less reliable Augustine seemed to understand it as being. This taxonomy, which is equally applicable to voices, was highly influential, being taken up in different ways by many later writers.

The biblical record itself is also apparently ambiguous, at least in relation to visions. In the prologue to John's Gospel, we read that 'No one has ever seen God', and yet, in Genesis, Jacob is said to have seen God 'face to face' and in Matthew's Gospel Jesus says that the pure in heart are blessed, 'for they will see God'.[2] Of course, nowhere is it said that 'No one has ever heard God', and it is important to distinguish between visions and voices, but this ambiguity persists through the post-biblical tradition in relation to all sensory-like experiences. Some Christians have always been cautious about placing too much weight on voices and visions.

The Desert Fathers and Mothers of the early church were certainly not unfamiliar with extraordinary experiences in prayer, at least judging from the evidence available to us.[3] Generally speaking, they seem to have sought 'imageless' (we might also say 'wordless') contemplation of God. Following in this tradition a millennium later, Walter Hilton was able to write that visions and 'any other sensible experiences of seemingly spiritual origin...do not constitute true contemplation'.[4] Like Augustine, Hilton understood the inner experience as being more important than the outer (corporeal) perception. John of the Cross, in the 16th century, identified no less than six kinds of harm that could arise as a result of placing too much weight on voices and, reflecting the Augustinian view, argued that 'The more exterior and corporeal these things are, the less certain is their divine origin'.[5] There thus came to be a view that the 'spiritual senses' are more important than the corporeal or imaginative.[6]

One of the main concerns within this cautionary tradition is the possibility of deception. We simply cannot be sure where voices or visions come from, or what they mean, and the human tendency is to

---

2 John 1.18; Genesis 32.30; Matthew 5.8, respectively.

3 Few of them left any written account of their teachings, a notable exception being Evagrius Pontus. Many of their sayings, or 'apophthegmata', passed on by oral tradition, were later written down and collected together. For a detailed account of the literature of the period, see Louth (2004).

4 Quoted in Sherley-Price (1988, p.10).

5 *The Ascent of Mount Carmel* 11.2. For an English translation, see Kavanaugh and Rodriguez (1991).

6 It has not always been clear exactly what the 'spiritual senses' are, and the matter is made no less confusing by the Augustinian distinction between 'spiritual' (imaginative) and 'intellectual' (we might say spiritual) in such a way that the latter is understood as more spiritual than the former. For a more detailed discussion, see Cook (2018, pp.210–213).

be too receptive to what we want to see or hear, and too deaf to what we do not want to hear. So great is this concern for John of the Cross that he recommends not spending time on thinking about what voices may have said, even if we think they did come from God. His one exception is what he calls 'substantial' voices. Such voices effect what they signify. Thus, if the voice says 'love me', it increases the love of the soul for God. John values these voices very highly indeed.[7] Apart from this, his approach seems to be simply to caution against giving too much attention to visions and voices.

Ignatian discernment

Ignatius Loyola, in the early 16th century, had similar concerns to John of the Cross in regard to the possibility of deception. However, he took a different approach to dealing with it. His *Spiritual Exercises* provided the basis for a process of discernment concerning vocation.[8] A recurring and foundational theme within the exercises is a concern with desire. For Ignatius, the fundamental human desire, the root of all other good desires, is the desire for God. We should therefore desire and choose only that which is conducive to the end for which we were created by God.[9] In practice, our desires are disordered; they proceed from what Ignatius referred to as the 'bad spirit', the enemy of human nature. Fundamentally, these disordered desires have their roots in selfishness, pride[10] and the denial of a creaturely relationship with God. The aim of the exercises is, through prayer and contemplation, the cultivation of our good desires and the conversion of disordered desires.[11]

---

7 *The Ascent of Mount Carmel* 11; see also the discussion in Cook (2018, p.129).

8 See Cook (2018, pp.124–127).

9 See 'Principle and Foundation of the Exercises', in Ivens and Hughes (2004, pp.11–12).

10 Here and elsewhere there is a patriarchal bias in the *Exercises*, and pride is arguably not the fundamental problem for women in the way that it is for men. Nor is it necessarily the fundamental problem for all men, but Ignatius clearly found that it was at the root of his own disordered desires.

11 For a helpful summary of the understanding of the nature of desire within the exercises, see Ivens and Munitiz (2007, pp.111–123).

Ignatius encourages the development of a form of prayer that he called colloquy. Colloquy is essentially a conversational form of prayer, in which the Christian is encouraged to approach God with concerns or questions and listen carefully to how God may respond. Whether in colloquy, on retreat or in the flow of daily life, the person undertaking the exercises is encouraged to discern the 'various movements produced in the soul' by good and bad 'spirits'.[12] Ignatius provides two sets of rules for discernment (summarized in Table 1), which show that he was very aware that feelings could be deceptive. His rules for working out whether good or bad forces were at work in the soul were particularly concerned with learning to identify experiences of consolation and desolation.

Consolation is essentially concerned with movement of the soul towards God. In consolation, the soul is inspired by love for God, finds herself growing in faith, hope and charity, and attracted to heavenly things. The soul in consolation is at peace, and finds interior happiness, but consolation should not simply be identified with happiness. The soul that finds herself in grief and tears when meditating on the passion of Christ, for example, is a soul in consolation. Desolation is the opposite of all of this. The soul finds herself in affective darkness, ill at ease, agitated, attracted to worldly things, and subject to temptation. Such a soul loses faith, hope and love. She is lazy, lukewarm and sad, feeling cut off from God. Again, such a state is not to be identified in any simplistic way with negative emotions. A place of much happiness (albeit superficial happiness, as Ignatius would understand it) could be a place of desolation in which the soul is absorbed in selfish and worldly pursuits and oblivious to heavenly things.

Ignatius provided two sets of rules for discernment, comprising 14 rules for those who are in the first week (or phase) of their retreat, and a further eight for those who are in the second week of their retreat (see Table 1). He shows himself aware of the subtle ways in

12 Whatever Ignatius may originally have understood here, most modern commentators understand these 'spirits' in primarily psychological terms, rather than as beings with ontological substance. They are the underlying causes of our deepest desires – whether for good (and thus ultimately the work of the Holy Spirit) or for bad (and thus, for one reason or another, disordered). See Ivens and Munitiz (2007, p.112).

which Christians who are in different places in the spiritual life might differently be tempted and deceived. For the beginner, guilt and remorse might be a sign of consolation. Thus, we might say, they might be the kinds of voices that we would expect a Christian to hear from God. For those who are making progress, however, the reverse may be true. Pangs of conscience, guilt or remorse may be voices of the bad spirit, which may actually impede progress in the spiritual life, causing the Christian to become bogged down in things that they have already been forgiven for.

Table 1: Summary of Ignatian rules for discernment

Week 1	Week 2
1. Conscience and remorse provoked by the good spirit 2. [*For those making progress*] Harassment, sadness and obstruction by the bad spirit; courage, strength, consolation, tears, inspiration and quiet from the good spirit 3. How to recognize consolation 4. How to recognize desolation 5. In time of desolation, stand by resolutions made in time of consolation 6. In time of desolation, pursue prayer, meditation, self-examination, penance 7. In time of desolation, resist temptation, drawing on divine grace even when it is not perceived 8. In time of desolation work at patience 9. Three principle causes for desolation: a. Faults (lukewarm, lazy, careless) b. Testing c. Knowledge and understanding of grace 10. In time of consolation, consider how to bear desolation 11. In time of consolation, develop humility and grace 12. Be bold and courageous in the face of temptation 13. Share difficult thoughts with a confessor or confidante 14. Identify vulnerability and weakness	1. God gives gladness and joy, and banishes sadness and distress 2. Consolation without preceding cause always comes from God 3. Consolation with cause can be deceptive 4. The bad angel assumes the form of an angel of light 5. Where do thoughts lead? 6. Where thoughts lead to an evil end, retrace them to learn from where they started 7. Contrary and similar dispositions of soul 8. Examine carefully experiences of consolation without preceding cause

The 'rules' are actually exercises in themselves. They provide instructions as to how one should act in times of consolation or desolation, they involve self-reflection, and they provide a programme of instruction to cultivate greater awareness of the spiritual significance of particular kinds and trains of thought and the impact that they have upon the human soul. The rules are not explicitly applied to 'voices', but the good and bad spirits identified within the exercises might easily be voices. The important consideration is not whether the thoughts are perception-like, or verbal, but rather the impact that they have upon the human soul in her relationship with God. The rules provide a helpful basis for questioning and challenging the voices that we hear.

As noted in the Introduction (Chapter 1), our inner voices do not speak to us directly about our desires, but rather about our beliefs. Their role in developing self-awareness about what we most desire is exercised through the part that they play in enabling self-reflection. The exercises effectively take advantage of this dynamic within a theological framework that asserts the place of God as the root of all good desires. Ignatius's good and bad 'spirits', within modern parlance, might well be understood as the good and bad voices that we hear within or (in the case of AVHs) without.

The Ignatian exercises have had broad influence within the Church. Arising within a Western Catholic tradition, they have been increasingly popular amongst Protestants too, and have given rise to a large popular literature.[13] The principles (if not the details of the rules) of Ignatian spirituality are used widely in retreat centres and in spiritual direction.

Charismatic discernment

Other kinds of rules for discernment are not always written down in such a systematic way as those left by Ignatius. Tanya Luhrmann (2012, p.63), in her book *When God Talks Back*, based on research in the Vineyard churches in North America, suggests that the rules, or tests,

13 Huggett (1990). See also, for example, Sheldrake (1991, 1998) and Silf (1998, 2004).

for knowing whether or not it was God that had spoken were more like 'the way teenagers know the local expectations of how to dress and date'. They are unspoken, but widely understood.

This has not stopped many authors from making their own written lists. Table 2 shows examples from four, fairly randomly selected, popular Christian books on this subject, alongside the criteria identified in the Vineyard communities by Luhrmann. While there is a lot of variability, there are also some common themes. Scripture as a source of authority is referenced in all but one of these lists. In the one case where scripture is not included as a helpful test, this is only because it has already been excluded as not often useful in practice:

> Many people teach that anything we believe we've heard from God must line up with scripture in order for us to know with certainty that it's from God. If it does not line up with scripture, they say, we must toss it out. There's nothing wrong with searching the scriptures to see if something has a biblical basis, but many of the things God will reveal to us cannot be verified by the scriptures. I've had God speak to me about accepting a new job, turning down opportunities to speak at various churches, and many other personal issues, none of which could be conclusively verified by scripture alone.[14]

There is also a strong consequentialist line of reasoning throughout these tests. Is the effect of the voice, or the outcome of what the voice may be suggesting, likely to bear good fruit? Is it associated with love, humility, peace, conviction of sin? These similarities aside, however, there is also a lot of variability. Only Joyce Huggett explicitly mentions the importance of critical application of the intellect. Some emphasize more the inner quality of the voice, or its subjective impact, and some give more attention to what other Christians think about the content of what the voice has said, or whether its message is corroborated externally. Both internal and external considerations are variably attended to. For example, if seeking confirmation from others, is it their critical judgement that is sought, or corroboration from their experiences of praying about the same thing?

14 Praying Medic (2017, p.55).

Table 2: Hearing God – Some Christian charismatic approaches to discernment

Huggett **(1986, pp.144–146)**	**Willard** **(1999, pp.166–174)**	**Luhrmann** **(2012, pp.63–65)**	**Williamson** **(2016, pp.118–126)**	**Praying Medic** **(2017, pp.53–57)**
1. Is the result of this piece of listening in alignment with scripture? 2. Do the circumstances substantiate what I heard? Has it come true? 3. Is my attitude Christ-like, characterized by humility, or is it reminiscent of Satan, the rebellious one? 4. Is this still, small voice prompting me or others to live in a way that honours God and obeys him, or will the suggestion bring his name and honour into question or disrepute? 5. Submit what I hear to others so that they can weigh the word…and determine its origin 6. Not to neglect my intellect but to sharpen the powers of my thinking	1. The quality of God's voice is more a matter of a certain *weight* or impact of the impression that its communications make on our consciousness 2. The voice of God speaking in our souls…is a spirit of exalted peacefulness and confidence, of joy, of sweet reasonableness, and of will for the good 3. The content of a word that is truly from God will always conform to, be consistent with, the truths about God's nature and Kingdom that are made clear in the Bible	1. The first test was whether what you had heard or imagined was the kind of thing you would say or imagine anyway: if it was, the thought was probably yours. If not, it could be God 2. The second test was whether it was the kind of thing God would say or imply. This was often articulated as making sure what you thought God had said did not contradict God's word in the Bible 3. The third test was whether the revelation could be confirmed through circumstances or through other people's prayers 4. The final test was the feeling of peace. Prayer and God's voice are thought to give you peace and comfort. If what you heard (or saw) did not, it did not come from God	1. Just don't expect inner peace 2. If any word conflicts with God's word (or to the degree that it conflicts), it isn't a word from God 3. Finding discernment in community 4. Get confirmation… When God is speaking to us he, usually, whispers. But it's a normally a persistent whisper 5. Expect periodic conviction of sin and idolatory… If God's words to us do not include frequent and precise convictions of sins, we must question whether we have learned to recognize God's voice 6. Learn to recognize the sound of God's voice… The more we hear his voice, the more we recognize it 7. Reflect on past experiences. We're not always right, but we can always learn 8. Peace has its role… When we finally do listen and obey, we get a sense that our obedience is right	1. God's thoughts are so much more sublime than my thoughts. They are full of love, life, wisdom, compassion, and mercy 2. A message that is external to us cannot be changed by us. Whereas a message that originates in our soul can be changed by exerting our will over it 3. The source of anything is always best determined by examining the fruit that it bears. False teachers and evil spirits can quote the scriptures, but the fruit that a thing produces will always reveal its source

The first problem, then, if not adopting the more dismissive approach of Walter Hilton or John of the Cross (whereby attention should simply not be given to voices and visions), is that judgements have to be made as to the reliability of the voice that has been heard. These judgements in turn require some kind of process, or a set of criteria, by which one may discriminate between good voices and bad voices. They either become exercises in evaluating evidence, exercises that rely heavily on human powers of reason, or they become somewhat anti-intellectual. Without wishing to caricature too much, the line of reasoning either becomes 'This sounds sensible – it must be God', or else 'This is not something that I would have thought...so it must be God'. Neither of these approaches is very satisfactory. The one takes everything back to an intellectual analysis based on human reason, and the other simply dismisses reason.

The second problem is that the experience of hearing thoughts that are 'not something I would have thought' is not unique to Christian experience. To some extent, almost everyone has experiences of this kind, as they imagine what others might think, or try to explore creative and different approaches to life's problems and challenges. In a more vivid way, writers of fiction find that the characters they have created develop a life of their own, so that they can almost hear them speaking and have access to their inner thoughts. These 'muses' were also ascribed to a divine source in the ancient classical world, whereas now they are more often understood as an inner creative source experienced by artists in non-religious terms. It might well be argued that Christians are simply ascribing similar experiences to God, but this does not necessarily mean that they *are* God. On the other hand, to some extent, at least, perhaps God is speaking to everyone in this way?

We are thus taken back to the fundamental problem of how to discern whether or not it is God that is speaking to us through our inner voices, or whether they come from elsewhere. However, it is not at all clear that it is necessary to create a big gulf of separation between human thoughts and divine inspiration. Why may human thoughts – things that I would have thought – not sometimes be inspired by God?

Thinking God's thoughts

The voices heard by contributors to this book were sometimes out loud, and sometimes more thought-like, but they were always relational. The experience was of a voice that was 'not me' addressing 'me' in a significant way – whether at a time of crisis or in everyday conversational prayer. The scientific research – both on inner voices and on AVHs – would suggest that this is not surprising. That is exactly how the thoughts that comprise our consciousness work. We have the capacity for an inner dialogue, an ability to create a place holder for thoughts or voices that we do not identify as our own. The sceptic might then say that this provides a basis on which to explain it all away. However, the sceptical argument only works while we retain a strong sense of demarcation between 'thoughts that are mine' contrasted with 'thoughts that are not mine'. What if the voice of God is actually an inspiration of my own – human – thoughts? This might be more like the model of the Old Testament prophet addressing the people of Israel. It was Ezekiel's voice that they heard – or Isaiah's, or Jeremiah's – but it was God who spoke *through* the prophet. It was not 'just' a human voice. Similarly, why should we not expect God to speak to us through our own, human, thoughts? Perhaps we might all, from time to time, have prophetically inspired thoughts? Of course, we might also have demonically inspired thoughts – rather like Jesus being tempted in the wilderness – but they would still be our thoughts, even though not 'just' our thoughts.

In the context of scholarship on Old Testament prophecy, it has been suggested that 'God does not speak Hebrew'.[15] Of course, in one sense, God speaks every language. He understands us all, from whatever culture or nation or background we come. However, that is not God 'speaking' a particular language; it is God listening, and understanding our language. If God has something to say, how does he communicate it to us? Given that we cannot ever fully comprehend the infinite reality that is God, a reality that ultimately transcends the words of any human language, how might he speak to us in terms that we can understand? I suggested in the Introduction (Chapter 1)

15 McKane (1995, pp.x, 145–146).

that the life, death and resurrection of Jesus are together the pivotal event of divine speech. In Jesus we hear the voice of God most clearly, and we hear it in relationship. We hear it in the relationship of the Father, Son and Holy Spirit, a relationship into which we are invited. We hear it in the human voice of Jesus in the Gospels. We hear it also as our hearts and minds respond to God in Christ. The answering voice within us is, at the same time, our own human voice, and also the eternal voice. However, as this voice becomes incarnate within our own thoughts, there is a process of translation, or interpretation, taking place. The voice is translated from God's language into ours. Whether our language is Hebrew, or English, or any other human tongue, that process of translation will involve interpretation, and in the process errors may creep in.

We are all familiar with the triumphs and pitfalls of social dialogue within one-to-one relationships, families, and communities. When we communicate well with one another, life tends to be happier for all concerned, but communication is fraught; we do not always communicate well. In a careless moment, I may easily and unintentionally say the wrong thing and cause pain or offence. Conversely, I may hear something other than what was said or intended and either be needlessly distressed, or else falsely reassured. We have to work at communication, both in thinking about what we say and in listening well. This is no less true in our relationship with God. The problem is not with divine speech, but with our ability to listen and interpret well, and in our hasty, careless, or ill-judged responses.

'Did God say that – or was it just my own thought?' This is probably the key question within this book, and answers to it are likely to depend heavily on spirituality and theological conviction. Tanya Luhrmann's assessment of the first test within the Vineyard communities[16] was concerned with whether or not what the voice said was something that I might have thought. If it was, then it was not God. Praying Medic's first principle is that God's thoughts are so much more sublime than human thoughts.[17] Both of these rules take as a starting point the

16 Luhrmann (2012).

17 Praying Medic (2017).

impact of sin on the human mind. God is good – but human beings are sinful. If I thought it, it can't be good. If God said it, it must be right. Whilst I understand the point, I suspect that it reflects, on the one hand, a pessimism influenced by Calvinism, and on the other hand, an optimism reflecting a particular charismatic theology. Why may my thoughts not be inspired by God? Why may I not make mistakes when hearing a voice that sounds 'other' than my own inner thoughts?

To take a particular example – if I feel compassion for the homeless, and think it would be good to set up a soup kitchen, does this thought have to be from God? It would be a sad thing indeed if I must imagine that I could never have such a good thought myself. Why should this not reflect my listening well to the voice of divine compassion for the poor? Why may the desire that lies behind this thought not be divinely implanted in my heart and mind? On the other hand, if I did have such a thought, perhaps it reflects any one of a number of traps or distortions of human thinking. Does it reflect sinful pride or hidden motives? Perhaps it is my way of avoiding other responsibilities, or my way of seeking approval from others? Perhaps it is my overcompensation for an only partly acknowledged inner revulsion about doing such a thing? The Desert Fathers were adept at managing such thoughts, and developed a variety of ways of dealing with them, but they did so on the premise that thoughts could be human – our own – as well as angelic or demonic. To ascribe all evil to ourselves does not help us to resolve the puzzle.

Dialogue with God

The dialogical nature of consciousness is such that thoughts can be at once my own thoughts – that is, within my own mind – and also not mine – that is, not reflecting what I most truly want. This can work both ways. I maybe don't have to feel so guilty about the bad thoughts, because I consciously reject them and they do not reflect what I most deeply desire. On the other hand, I perhaps should not feel so good about the good thoughts, because I have not yet fully owned them or put them into action. The wisdom of the Desert Fathers, and the beauty of the Ignatian exercises, is that they have each devised their own ways to get to the bottom of all of this. The Ignatian exercises are fundamentally about exploring what we most deeply desire. The Desert Fathers were good at exposing unpresentable motives.

I think that the fundamental key to all of this is not, however, the unravelling of the puzzle of human thoughts. The key is to be found in the relationality of the ongoing encounter with God in Christ. Do we encounter God in the voice? The relationality of the inner voices that form the milieu of human consciousness echoes (and, due to sin, also distorts) the relationality within the God who is encountered as the Father, Son and Holy Spirit. We encounter Christ – if we encounter him at all – within the dialogue, rather than in any particular word or sentence. Perhaps my thought about the soup kitchen is partly mine, and partly God's? In the process of prayerful reflection – perhaps on a retreat, or during my daily prayers, or at a celebration of the Eucharist in church – I may become aware of both the good and the bad motives that lie behind the thought. My contemplation of the prospect of following through with my plans may lead me to a place of greater consolation or desolation, within which I may become more aware of my own deeper desires. If all goes well, I get to know myself and God better as a result of the conversation.

Of course, as in human relationships, not all conversations go well. The outcome may be that I deceive myself about the truth, that I move away from God, or that I attribute my inner voices to God when they are actually not divinely inspired at all. Whilst this would be, in Ignatian terms, desolation, I may not acknowledge it as such. I may consciously consider myself to be a very spiritual person. I may think myself very wise. I may consider myself 'happy' and blessed. The possibility of self-deception is very real. It is in giving an account of ourselves to another in spiritual direction, or on a guided retreat, that we have the opportunity for critical self-examination designed to identify such a possibility. Even then, we may not be completely sure that we have heard God well. However, as we follow through on what we have heard, in the outworking of subsequent events, the true value of what we have discerned may become clear. This is one of the reasons why Ignatius considered the daily examination of conscience so important. Discernment is an ongoing process, not a one-off decision.

Whilst conversation is a good model for understanding the voices that Christians hear, it also has its limitations. As stories in various chapters of this book have shown (especially some of the earlier chapters), a voice may be not so much a part of a dialogue but more an intervention, an interruption, or a turning point. Occurring perhaps just once in a lifetime, and bringing about a radical change, or else offering instruction or reassurance at a crucial moment of crisis, the voice may be more of a breakthrough, a signal, or a sign of something important that is taking place. It is not so much part of a dialogue as a command or statement. What has been said by the voice may still be the cause for ongoing reflection – as in the case of Julian's reflections over two decades on the revelations that she received as a young woman. However, it does not so much require a conversational reply as a change of life. Sometimes, as with voices identified by John of the Cross as 'substantial', the voice actually seems to bring about the change, or at least to be an accompaniment to a change brought about by God. In such cases, the crucial test of authenticity would seem to be that of the fruit that they bear. Do they give life or instil faith? Do they bring about better, holier, lovelier lives?

Evil voices

Some of the voices reported in this book, notably in Chapter 11, would seem unambiguously evil. They certainly were not pleasant to hear. What part does discernment play here? It would be easy to dismiss such voices as the opposite of all that is good, and thus not to be listened to, and this would certainly sometimes seem to be the case. However, that does not mean that they are never meaningful. They may bring to the attention of consciousness traumatic memories of things past that are not so much untrue but, rather, in need of healing. Failure to attend to such voices may impede healing and growth. They may put into words deeply seated fears which, although not true, may still be indicators that all is not well. We need to pay heed to such voices, albeit giving too much attention to what they mean may be as painful and unhelpful as attempting to ignore them completely. Helpful responses to such voices might include trauma-informed psychological therapies (see Chapter 14). In Chapter 12, Rachel tells her story of how a combination of spiritual and psychological interventions, along with the support of her family and friends, brought about a process of healing.

What about the voices that are not helpful reminders of the wounds that need healing; the voices that, rather, seem to speak with evil intention? If questions arise for Christians as to whether some voices are from God, then corresponding questions may arise as to whether some voices are demonic, but what does it mean to say that a voice is 'demonic'? Whilst mainstream psychiatry has almost entirely medicalized such voices as due to illness, Christians are more divided about what to think. Some, adopting a more medical or scientific approach, would see such voices in terms of our contemporary knowledge of psychological processes, including scientific research on AVHs.[18] Other Christians perceive demonic voices as evidence of a more ontologically-based model of demons as personal, non-material evil entities that have the power to assail and afflict human beings.[19] Yet others might adopt elements of both approaches.[20] The decision that is taken concerning the relative merits of these approaches is likely to dictate the form of intervention that is offered. On the one hand, referral may be offered to mental health services, and on the other, deliverance ministry or exorcism may be offered within the churches. The relative merits and demerits of these different responses will be explored in the next chapter. First, however, it is necessary to consider further what it might mean to say that a voice is 'demonic'.

In the New Testament, it is only Jesus who clearly hears the voice of Satan, and only the Gospels of Matthew and Luke provide any detail in their narrative concerning this. We are not told whether the voice is 'out loud' or an inner voice. At his baptism, Jesus hears a voice affirming that he is God's son.[21] Immediately afterwards, in the desert, he hears a voice questioning what this means: 'If you are God's son…' the voice

18 Wilson (1975).

19 See, for example, Dow (1980); Irmak (2014); and Isaacs (1987).

20 Dunn and Twelftree (1980).

21 In Matthew, the voice is addressed to the crowd rather than to Jesus. In Mark and Luke it is addressed directly to Jesus, although Luke leaves open the possibility that it was also heard by the crowd.

says, then 'do this…' The things that the voice proposes challenge Jesus to consider what form his vocation as God's son will take. In each case, Jesus has to consider whether the voice is the same one that he heard at his baptism. Should it be trusted? Should it be obeyed? In each case, Jesus decides that it should not be trusted or obeyed. The voice offers an understanding of vocation that is self-serving rather than God-serving. As Ignatius might have said, it is a voice of desolation, not consolation. However, the voice helps Jesus to discern what he should do. Paradoxically, it assists him in discerning his divinely given vocation. There is absolutely no suggestion that it provided evidence that Jesus was possessed by demons.[22] If Jesus was spirit possessed, then he was possessed by the Holy Spirit.[23]

All three Synoptic Gospels (Matthew, Mark and Luke) provide accounts of Jesus's work as an exorcist. The people from whom Jesus casts out unclean spirits and demons would probably now be diagnosed as suffering from epilepsy or other neurological conditions, and do not give the appearance of people who were hearing voices.[24] Epilepsy, mutism and blindness are generally understood by Christians as reasons for medical referral, not deliverance ministry. Only the Gerasene demoniac[25] might appear to resemble the presentation of

22 Jesus's critics do, of course, suggest that he is possessed (Mark 3.22; John 7.20; 8.48–52; 10.20). However, this is clearly not based on Jesus's experiences of temptation in the wilderness, about which they appear to know nothing.

23 See Davies (2014) for a detailed discussion.

24 In the case of the spirit of the unclean demon exorcised in Mark 1.21–28 and Luke 4.33–36, and the exorcism of the daughter of the Syrophoenecian woman (Matthew 15.21–28; Mark 7.24–30), too little information is given to enable any clear diagnosis. The boy with convulsions, whose exorcism by Jesus is recorded in all three Synoptic Gospels (Matthew 17.14–21; Mark 9.14–29; Luke 9.37–43) would appear to have had epilepsy. The dumb demoniac (Matthew 9.13–24), the man with the mute demon (Luke 11.14–26), and the blind and mute demoniac (Matthew 12.22–24) would all appear to have had some kind of neurological condition or disability. Only the Gerasene demoniac (Mark 5.1–20; Luke 8.26–39) may have had a mental disorder. Mark and Luke refer to him as being 'in his right mind' after Jesus cast the unclean spirits out of him. There is no clear evidence that he was hearing voices, although some commentators do speculate that he was suffering from a psychotic condition.

25 Matthew 8.28–34; Mark 5.1–20; Luke 8.26–39. In Matthew's account there are two men, rather than one, but much less detail concerning their condition.

someone suffering from psychosis, but there is no evidence within the Gospel texts to suggest that he was hearing voices. A case can therefore be made for the demythologization of all of the exorcism narratives in favour of contemporary medical and scientific understanding.

In the early church, and in the Eastern Christian tradition, there is continuing reference to the demonic affliction of human beings. Sometimes (as in the case of Antony of Egypt), it may be asserted that the hearing of demonic voices seems to provide one element of the presenting picture. However, the relationships between human thoughts, passions, vices and demonic activity are complex and paradoxical. In the writings of Evagrius, for example, there is a tension between the extent to which they are understood as internal rather than external forces; something for which people are responsible, rather than something that assails them from without, against their will.[26] In our terms, this understanding of demonology might be said to be much more psychological than ontological. It accords much more readily with the narratives of Jesus's temptation in the wilderness than it does with the Gospel exorcism narratives. For Augustine of Hippo, evil was understood as an absence, or corruption, of the good, having no substance in itself.[27] For Barth, evil was understood to exist only in negativity, in opposition to God, or as 'Nothingness'.[28] According to this kind of understanding, demons may be understood not so much as spiritual beings that 'possess' people as 'non-beings', evil ideas, negations and perversions of all that is good. Giving voice to such things may be demonic, but, in this sense at least, the existence of demonic voices does not necessarily imply the existence of non-corporeal spiritual entities.

In the contemporary medical literature, belief in demon possession is recognized as a component of the psychopathology associated with

---

26 See Cook (2011b, pp.54–57). Anticipating Ignatius's concept of desolation, there is a theme within Evagrius which understands the passions or demons as states of mind that bring about separation from God; they impede prayer, they enslave us, they foster human pride.

27 See, for example, *Confessions* 7.XII.

28 For a helpful essay drawing on Barth and other sources, see Wright (2011).

some mental disorders. For example, in David Enoch and Hadrian Ball's *Uncommon Psychiatric Syndromes*, it is stated:

> A possession state can be defined as the presence of a belief, delusional or otherwise, held by an individual (and sometimes by others) that their symptoms, experiences and behaviour are under the influence or control of supernatural forces, often of diabolical origin.[29]

Possession is a culturally shaped concept and on a worldwide basis possession may represent the commonest culture-bound psychiatric syndrome.[30] Possession states do not necessarily involve the hearing of voices, but sometimes they do.[31] Nor is belief in possession necessarily evidence of mental illness. An Australian survey of 126 mentally healthy Protestant Christians revealed that over a third believed that mental illness might be caused by demon possession.[32] A similar proportion of psychiatric outpatients in Switzerland (also mainly Protestant Christians) believed that their symptoms could possibly be caused by evil spirits, either through 'bondage' or possession.[33] In another study, of 33 members of a US Vineyard church, 70 per cent indicated that they had at some time or another felt certain that a demonic presence

---

29 Enoch and Ball (2001, pp.224–244). The definition quoted here may be found on p.224.

30 Littlewood (2004).

31 In one early account of demonomania, it was noted that, 'Some hear [the devil] speak, and his voice proceeds from the stomach, bowels or uterus. They converse with him, the devil recommending to them the commission of crimes, murders, acts of incendiarism and suicide... He threatens and even strikes them if they do not obey his orders' (Esquirol 1845, p.246). In a group of 16 patients who believed that they were possessed, Whitwell and Barker (1980) reported that hallucinations were 'common symptoms' but did not provide any further information as to the nature of these hallucinations. Goff *et al.* (1991) compared 25 psychotic patients with delusions of possession with 36 patients not having such delusions. Patients believing that they were possessed were more likely to report auditory hallucinations and more likely to hear voices inside their heads. Unfortunately, the paper does not identify whether or not patients heard specifically demonic voices. For reports of individual cases in which people who were said to be possessed heard demonic voices, see Schendel and Kourany (1980) (case 5), Maniam (1987) (case 2) and Peck (2005).

32 Hartog and Gow (2005).

33 Pfeifer (1994).

was near at hand.[34] Hearing the voice of the Devil appears to be more commonly associated with psychosis than with the religious experience of mentally healthy Christians.[35] However, in one study of 124 female university students,[36] subjects who reported spiritual visions or voices scored significantly higher on a scale of 'diabolical experiences' (including experiences of evil presence, being 'overtaken' by this presence, being under the control of Satan, etc.).

One of the earliest psychological studies of possession, *Possession Demoniacal and Other among Primitive Races, in Antiquity, the Middle Ages, and Modern Times*,[37] identified three consistent manifestations of possession: a change of physiognomy, a change of voice, and a speaking of the new voice as though it were a new personality. The author, Traugott Oesterreich, concluded that the changed voice associated with possession:

> ...is essentially the same as when I converse mentally with someone and in imagination hear him reply, by which means a conversation may be enacted...
>
> In the case of possession there is nothing more than an extraordinary accentuation of this phenomenon. Instead of the discussion being purely and simply a figment of the imagination, there is simultaneous compulsive excitement of the vocal organs and eventually yet other actions of a compulsive nature.[38]

This understanding accords remarkably well with contemporary scientific theories of voice hearing, but is it appropriate to reduce such phenomena to scientific frameworks of explanation? It has been argued, on both empirical and theological grounds, that forms of possession may be identified which are distinguishable from those associated with conventional psychiatric diagnoses. In a widely cited text, John Richards (1939–2011), a member of the Bishop of Exeter's Study Group on Exorcism, argued that Christians should:

---

34 Cassaniti and Luhrmann (2014).

35 Cottam *et al.* (2011).

36 Spanos and Moretti (1988).

37 Oesterreich (1930).

38 Oesterreich (1930, p.65).

> ...not relegate the demonic solely to -isms and -ologies with which [they] disagree...[39]

He further argued that demons:

> ...are spirit-beings with intelligence and malevolence. They are not mere forces, or urges...[40]

Whilst demonic possession clearly presents with features familiar to psychiatrists, critics argue that conventional diagnostic criteria do not adequately characterize it, and that it can be distinguished from these diagnoses.[41] It has even been argued that it is possible to distinguish voices that are due to schizophrenia from those that are due to possession.[42] The latter are said to be characterized by content that is opposed to the Christian faith.[43]

In an influential book by the Christian Deliverance Study Group of the Church of England, hallucinations were identified as characteristic of so-called 'false possession', understood as a possession syndrome due to major mental illness and, therefore, not due to the activity of an evil spiritual or demonic influence.[44] In the same book, voices and hallucinations were not explicitly included amongst signs of what

39 Richards (1974, p.151).

40 Richards (1974, p.151).

41 Isaacs (1987); Lhermitte (1963); and Sall (1976).

42 Koch (1971, pp.163–164).

43 In the same book, it is also argued that patients with mental ill health are more likely to express the belief that they are possessed, whereas those who are truly possessed will not mention demons (Richards 1974, p.162). Criteria of this kind, which do not appear to be based on any empirical research, are difficult to evaluate, but they are not argued from primarily scientific premises. They reflect, rather, an attempt to amalgamate certain theological and scientific models of understanding, allowing each its own domain of validity.

44 Perry (1996, pp.109–110). Millard Sall (1976), a clinical psychologist who sought to distinguish between demon possession and psychopathology, understood hallucinations as characteristic of the latter, thus providing an indication that the person was not possessed. Martin Israel, a pathologist and Anglican priest, also seems to have understood hallucinations as primarily associated with schizophrenia or another mental disorder. However, he also keeps open the possibility that someone might be suffering from mental disorder as well as subject to 'demonic attack' (Israel 1997, pp.85–90).

we might call 'genuine' demonic oppression or possession. However, people suffering from demonic oppression 'when given spiritual advice or when in contact with spiritual objects' are said to experience 'vile suggestions' that come into their minds.[45] People suffering from demonic possession, immediately before exorcism is about to be undertaken, are said to 'see and/or hear demonic and terrible figures speaking, and threatening [them]'.[46] The Christian Deliverance Study Group therefore seemed to recognize a degree of complexity concerning the significance and interpretation of voices.

The ontological question, concerning the supposed nature or substance of demonic entities, may actually not be as important in practice as many seem to suppose.[47] Chris MacKenna,[48] an Anglican priest, Jungian analyst and diocesan advisor on deliverance ministry with many years' experience, has shown in a series of case studies that a multiprofessional and multidisciplinary approach is almost always required in practice – a consideration to which we shall return in the next chapter. In fact, most of the cases presented by MacKenna do not seem to involve the hearing of voices. Nor is it clear that the hearing of voices in any way distinguishes particular types or sub-types of demonic influence that need to be treated differently.

Returning to our question of what it might mean to say that a voice is 'demonic', there is clearly a variety of possible answers. For some, it will usually or always mean that there is identifiable psychopathology, or else that there are culturally shaped beliefs in possession within which the hearing of a voice is to be understood. From such a perspective, medical and psychological, rather than spiritual, interventions will primarily be indicated but, even then, the importance of the cultural perspective is such that some would argue that exorcism might still sometimes be appropriate as an 'exotic' form of treatment.[49] For others,

45 Israel (1997, p.123).

46 Israel (1997, p.124).

47 It is beyond the scope of this book to explore this question in any detail. For further discussion, see Barton (2008); Dow (1980); and Dunn and Twelftree (1980).

48 MacKenna (2013).

49 Leff (1975).

the possibility remains that there is something distinguishable from psychopathology, an objective and personal manifestation of evil. According to advocates of this stance, some people will need medical interventions and others will need spiritual interventions. Some might go one step further, and argue that schizophrenia and its associated auditory verbal hallucinations are often (perhaps even usually?) due to demonic influence.[50]

It is beyond the scope of this book to resolve this debate, but the challenge for Christian discernment will be to ensure that neither the psychological nor spiritual aspects of the experience are ignored or over-simplified. Rather than a crude dualism, within which spiritual and psychological domains are understood as boundaried and distinguishable, it is proposed here that the spiritual dimension is to be addressed in the very midst of the bio-psycho-social matrix within which human lives are lived. It is an over-simplification, and a mis-representation, of the relationship between the science and theology of demonic voices and demon possession to suggest that under a psychological model demons 'do not exist'. As all who work in mental health services know only too well, the things that we believe, our affects and emotions, and the voices that we hear, are all very real experiences. On the other hand, as Augustine asserted long ago, evil – though very real – has no substance. In the next chapter, we shall consider the most appropriate spiritual, pastoral and clinical interventions.

Voices: Human, demonic and divine

Voices – whether they are out loud, or more like our own thoughts – may be human, demonic or divine. In one sense, they will always be human, because they are heard by human minds. However, they may also be human in the sense that they are things that 'I' thought, and they reflect what I believe, what I want, or what I don't want. They may be human in the sense that I know they came from other people who are important to me. I recognize that the voice within is the voice of

50 Irmak (2014).

my father. I can just imagine him saying something like that. Human thoughts arise from a variety of sources, many of which we are not fully aware of, many of which may be emotionally significant, but which are, nonetheless, a characteristically human affair. My proposal here, in keeping with Christian scripture and tradition, and in line with the experience of my contributors, is that some voices are not only this. Voices may also be demonic or divine. However, they cannot always be taken at face value. The apparently demonic voice may be a traumatic consequence of sexual abuse, warning me that I need help. The apparently divine voice may reflect merely what I would like God to be saying, an avoidance of God's actual demands on my life. The thought that seems like 'my' idea may be divinely inspired, the voice of God within, prompting me, changing me and challenging me to fulfil my unique and God-given Christian vocation.

Discernment of the voices that Christians hear may thus be complex. It may sometimes be easy to get things wrong, to be misled, but in other cases it may be 'the voice' that puts life back on track. Voices take the guise of evil, and may say things that Christians do not want to hear, or they may sound seductively good, flattering us with what we do want to hear. Discernment requires humility, wisdom and a willingness critically to explore different possible interpretations.

Chapter 14

Clinical and Pastoral Practice

The majority of contributors to this book neither needed nor sought clinical or pastoral help in relation to their experiences of hearing a voice. The notable exceptions, primarily in Chapters 7, 10, 11 and 12, concerned voices in the context of mental disorder, the sequelae of sexual abuse, and voices that were evil and/or distressing. However, any of the experiences recorded in other chapters might have later become a matter for conversation with a priest, counsellor or other helping professional. Stephen (in Chapter 6) reflects on how he, as a psychotherapist, might understand his own experience of hearing a voice in psychological as well as spiritual terms. Mary (in Chapter 6) and Lucy (in Chapter 7) each express their reluctance to talk about their experiences for fear of whether others will doubt their sanity. As explored in Chapter 13, voices speak into critical theological debates concerning spiritual discernment. There are thus many ways in which the voices that Christians hear raise significant questions for pastoral or clinical practice. The present chapter seeks to explore practical answers to some of these questions.

Before moving on to focus on the complex, the problematic and the difficult aspects of the topic, it is important, however, to affirm the positive. The majority of stories told by contributors to this book give testimony to an experience of an encounter with God that was both life enriching and encouraging for Christian faith. Keith (in Chapter 2) relates that the 'six life-changing words' that he heard almost 30 years ago have made him not so much happier as more purposeful. All of the stories related in Chapter 3 concern voices that positively changed the course of lives and vocations. The voices of Chapter 4, all occurring in the context of life or death crises, gave hope and life. The voices of Chapter 5 provided comfort amidst adversity, and those of Chapter 6 gave confirmation and clarification amidst uncertainty. Voices are not just voices; they have agency and are associated with a sense of presence. For the contributors to this book, that agency variously provided a sense of protection and changed things for the better; the presence was one of divine comfort and encouragement. Even in some of the cases where the voices were distressing or unpleasant, the eventual outcome was a positive one. As Rachel notes (in Chapter 12):

> Whilst I am not defined by my trauma, voice or illness, I am defined by the fight I've fought to work through these things, and by the God I've found in the process. Had I not been on this journey, I wouldn't be the person I am today...

Getting help

Christians who hear voices are likely to find that there is no 'one-stop shop' at which they can find all the help that they may need. This book has focused primarily on spiritually significant voices, and the customary sources of spiritual wisdom and support may well not be the best places to get advice on mental health matters, or on voice hearing. Conversely, mental health services and support networks for people who hear voices may not always be places within which Christians may feel that they can seek spiritual guidance concerning their experiences. Most of the Christians who contacted me in the course of my research were not mentally ill and did not consider themselves to be voice hearers.

In charismatic Christian circles such as those represented by the Vineyard churches studied by Tanya Luhrmann in her research, the voices that are heard in prayer usually have nothing to do with mental disorder and are not identified as 'voice hearing' either. They are simply understood as experiences of God responding to prayer within an environment in which such things are both expected and encouraged. Even outside these circles, as the stories included in this book show, most Christian experiences of hearing voices are not identified by those who have them as experiences of 'hearing voices'. They are not evidence of vulnerability to psychosis. Some of them are part of the process of learning to pray or, as Luhrmann has suggested, 'The art of hearing God.'[1] Others are concerned with Christian reflection on vocation, or with crises and turning points at which things could have gone horribly wrong but – in God's providence – they did not. Help might therefore more appropriately be sought within spiritual direction, or in discussion with a priest or pastor, than in counselling, mental health services or the hearing voices network.

On the other hand, the voices that are heard by some Christians in the course of mental illness, or following trauma, may be both unexpected and unwelcome. Distressing voices are more likely to be associated with a psychiatric diagnosis, and those who experience them are thus likely to come into contact with mental health services. Whilst chaplains working in a mental health setting may be familiar with such phenomena, and well placed to provide pastoral care, the clinical team responsible for medical care may find the faith dimension both unfamiliar and difficult to understand. The so-called 'religiosity gap' between mental health professionals and their patients is concerned not only with the greater likelihood that the former will be atheist or agnostic and the latter affirming of faith, but also with the controversies surrounding good practice in relation to spirituality and religion in psychiatric practice.[2] Liaison between clinical teams and chaplaincy, usually affirmed in theory, is often not as close as it might be in practice. The gap between health service staff and clergy in the wider community is even bigger.

---

1 Luhrmann (2005, 2017); Luhrmann *et al.* (2013).

2 Concerning the 'religiosity gap', see Cook (2011a). Concerning controversies surrounding practice, see Cook (2013a). A number of national and international policy statements have now affirmed the place of spirituality or religion in good psychiatric practice (see Cook 2017c; Poole, Cook and Higgo 2019).

Giving help

Given the wide range of experiences that Christians hearing voices may have, it is difficult to offer universal rules for helping those who have them. If someone is seeking help, it is likely that there is some aspect of the experience that has been difficult or problematic, but they may just be seeking reassurance. In either case, the power imbalance between the pastor or clinician and the person who has made themselves vulnerable in sharing their experience should not be ignored. General principles that apply to all pastoral work, concerning safeguarding, confidentiality and compassionate care, all apply here as they do elsewhere.[3] Standards of good practice that govern professional work similarly apply in the healthcare context.[4]

A key matter for clarification will be the agenda of the person seeking help. They may simply require reassurance that they are not 'going mad'. On the other hand, they may be exploring questions of discernment and meaning, such as those explored in Chapter 13 of this book. They may be very aware of the gap between their own interpretation of their experience and the responses of those around them – in their family, church or society – who have not had that experience themselves. They may wish to persuade others of a truth that they believe God has imparted, and the pastor or clinician may be amongst those who are doubtful about that truth. Such a situation easily sets the scene for an unhelpful confrontation or conflict that helps no one. On the other hand, it potentially opens up a shared exploration of a significant spiritual experience that might be for the

3 See, for example, Litchfield (2006). People who hear voices are more likely to have experienced sexual abuse as children. Where disclosures of abuse are made, these should be handled according to good professional practice, observing the relevant legal requirements. Training on safeguarding procedures is mandatory for Church of England clergy and all clinical professionals working within the NHS. It is assumed that all professional readers, including clergy, chaplains and clinical staff working in a health context, will be familiar with their own obligations and with appropriate practice and procedures. However, safeguarding is not only the responsibility of professionals. For advice on how to handle such matters within a parish context in the Church of England, see House of Bishops of the Church of England (2019).

4 See, for example, Cook (2013b).

good of the person concerned and others. I have felt privileged to receive the stories related in this book, and others beside, and I treat them as holy ground, whether or not I agree with the interpretations of those who shared them.

Some specific principles of working with Christians (and others) who seek help concerning their experiences of hearing spiritually significant voices might include the following:

1. *The person who heard the voice is the expert on their own experience.* Interest in understanding that experience better is rarely unwelcome and can provide a good basis for building a better understanding of why someone feels about it as they do. As with all pastoral and clinical work, listening well is the starting point and foundation stone for good practice.

2. *Different interpretations should be respected.* Interpretation of spiritual experiences can be controversial and contentious. Whilst any good pastor or clinician should retain the integrity of their own view, and should tell the truth about this if asked, the interpretation of the voice by the person hearing the voice should be listened to and respected, in context, on its own terms.

3. *Questioning is helpful; confrontation is not.* A confrontational stance is rarely likely to be productive. Where the need arises, it is better to adopt a questioning approach. What do others say about this experience? What other possible interpretations might there be? What other thoughts have you had about what this voice might mean?

4. *Pay attention to feelings.* Attention not only to the voice, but to the affective experience of hearing the voice, is important. How did it make you feel? How do others feel about what you have told them? Has this been a positive experience, or a negative one? Has the hearing of this voice made you feel closer to God, or more distant?

5. *Discernment takes time.* Meaning is important. However, discernment of what God might be saying, or what the voice means, will rarely be a matter to be settled immediately. The general principles of discernment discussed in Chapter 13 may be helpful, but thoroughly working through them is likely to be a matter for ongoing spiritual direction or perhaps something to explore on retreat. Discernment takes time, and the full significance of the voices heard by some of the contributors to this book only became clear after many years.

6. *Reassurance has professional boundaries.* Reassurance is good when it can be provided, but it is important not to go beyond one's own expertise. Excluding the possibility of psychiatric disorder is the domain of mental health professionals and, where there is serious concern about this possibility, should precede any discussion of spiritual discernment, deliverance ministry or important life decisions. Reassurance that deliverance ministry is not needed will usually be provided by a priest or pastor with experience in such matters.
7. *Collaborative working is nearly always helpful, and essential sometimes.* In complex cases, especially where there is significant spiritual and psychological distress, or where questions concerning deliverance or exorcism arise, liaison between mental health professionals and chaplains or clergy is likely to be essential. Not all cases are complex, and sometimes multidisciplinary care will be sequential, not concurrent. However, it is important always to be mindful of the limits of one's own expertise, and open to the different perspectives and contributions that other professionals might bring.

Where there is evidence of psychiatric disorder, the appropriate treatment will depend on the diagnosis. AVHs may be associated with a wide range of different diagnoses, including borderline personality disorder, dissociative identity disorder, post-traumatic stress disorder, schizophrenia, bipolar disorder, depression, substance use disorders, dementia, Parkinson's disease and complex epilepsy.

Pastors and clinicians hearing voices

A category of voices that raises particular ethical and professional concerns is that of the voice heard by the clinician or pastor that speaks about matters relating to their work as a helping professional. Such voices may also be heard by other Christians – in a non-professional capacity – but clergy and members of the helping professions have a particular set of responsibilities to observe – towards their employers or churches, towards bodies governing professional standards, and, most of all, toward those for whom they care. What weight should they place, if any, on the voice that tells them something about a person for whom they are caring?

Two such examples may be found in this book. In Chapter 3, the voice that Liz hears tells her that it is the woman to whom she is speaking (and not that woman's husband) who should be ordained. In Chapter 5, Lucy, a doctor, hears a voice while praying that tells her that one of her patients is 'with angels'. Initially she does not know what this means, but almost immediately after hearing the voice she discovers that the patient has died. She tells the family of the patient about her experiences, and it is a comfort to them. Liz and Lucy have very different professional responsibilities. Liz, as a priest, would reasonably be expected to address questions of what God might be saying and to prayerfully explore them with those to whom she provides counsel. As a Diocesan Director of Ordinands (DDO), she also occupies a particular role within the Church of England with responsibility to her bishop for helping people to explore their possible vocations to ordained ministry. Lucy, in contrast, is expected to provide primarily medical care. However, working (as she was) in palliative care, she would reasonably be expected to recognize the important spiritual needs of patients and families at the end of life.[5] Whereas Liz shared a common faith with the woman with whom she was talking, Lucy and her patient's family belonged to different faith traditions.

For clergy, it is often implicit within a particular congregation or church tradition that 'voices' might be dealt with in a particular way. As Tanya Luhrmann has perceptively observed, it is understood in much the way that the rules for dating are understood by teenagers.[6] A rule book is neither necessary nor helpful! However, the rules can be very different in one church and another, and different theological traditions have very different approaches to how such experiences should be dealt with. The possibilities for misunderstanding must be particularly great where clergy find themselves ministering in a church context with which they are unfamiliar, or in churches (such as the Church of England) that encompass a very broad range of different traditions and theologies. There are also some rules that are fundamental. Just as mutual consent is of first importance in

---

5 See, for example, Asgeirsdottir *et al.* (2013) and Puchalski *et al.* (2009).

6 Luhrmann (2012).

dating, consent is foundational to pastoral work. Pastors should not impose their approach, including their theology, on those in their care who may have legitimately different views but less knowledge and confidence with which to articulate them.

For clinical staff working in the health services, professional guidance concerning good practice will usually be available in written form, and is likely to vary from one country or profession to another. The General Medical Council, for example, provides guidance for doctors registered in the UK that states that:

> You may talk about your own personal beliefs only if a patient asks you directly about them, or indicates they would welcome such a discussion. You must not impose your beliefs and values on patients, or cause distress by the inappropriate or insensitive expression of them.[7]

When such beliefs are shared, caution is urged concerning the importance of respecting the professional boundaries that maintain trust between doctor and patient. It would seem likely that the sharing with a patient, by a doctor, of an experience of hearing a voice would be seen to fall within the province of this guidance. The example provided by Lucy (which took place outside the UK) is notable for the comfort that it provided to the family of her patient. Where there might be potential for causing distress, or breaching boundaries, or where there is any doubt about how this disclosure might be received, the physician would be well advised to err on the side of caution and not share their experience with patient or family. Where such experiences are shared, good practice would require that this be recorded in the medical records and discussed in clinical supervision or with an appropriate senior colleague.[8]

---

7 General Medical Council (2013b, para.31).

8 Similar considerations arise here as in the contentious matter of praying with patients. See Poole and Cook (2011). Arguably, where a conversation with a patient strays onto such matters as what the clinician believes God may be saying, the conversation has become a kind of prayer, paying attention as it does to the relationships between God, patient and clinician.

Clinical treatment of auditory verbal hallucinations

As discussed in the Introduction (Chapter 1), AVHs may or may not be experienced in the context of mental illness. Those that are, are much more likely to be distressing and associated with negative affect. Those that are not, are much less likely to need 'treatment'. The focus in this section is therefore on the former, and in particular on voices in psychosis. In each case, the primary treatment is that appropriate to the underlying diagnosis. Whilst the range of diagnoses concerned includes in particular affective psychoses and schizophrenia, voices may also be heard in a range of other mental disorders, including borderline personality disorder, dissociative identity disorder and dementia. Voices may also be heard in the context of certain neurological disorders, including Parkinson's disease and complex forms of epilepsy.

The mainstay of treatment for AVHs in the context of psychosis has traditionally been pharmacological. A variety of drugs is available, and evidence suggests that they are usually highly effective. For patients diagnosed with a first episode of schizophrenia, a marked reduction in severity is usually achieved within one month. Only 8 per cent continue to experience hallucinations after a year of treatment. In addition, cognitive behavioural therapy (CBT) may be effective in reducing distress associated with the voices.[9] As evidence for the benefits of CBT in psychosis accumulates, some would argue that the research now warrants use of psychological therapies as the treatment of choice, with pharmacological treatment providing augmentation where necessary.[10] Hallucination-focused integrative treatment (HIT) offers an integrative approach combining both pharmacological and psychological therapies.[11]

A variety of newer therapies show promise. Taking a biological approach to the problem, stimulation of the left temporo-parietal region of the brain, using a magnetic field or weak electrical current,

9 Sommer *et al.* (2012).

10 Corstens *et al.* (2013).

11 Jenner (2016).

appears to reduce frequency or severity of AVHs for some individuals.[12] Taking a psychological approach, trauma-focused therapy seeks to better understand the relationship between trauma and voices and to use this as a basis for devising appropriate psychotherapeutic interventions.[13]

Various therapeutic strategies have been employed in order to alter the relationship between the voice hearer and their voice. Mindfulness and related therapies (notably, Acceptance and Commitment Therapy) may help to make voices less believable, less distressing and less interfering.[14] Voice dialoguing aims to break the destructive pattern of communication between voice hearer and voice, to enable better understanding of the voice, and to give the voice hearer more control.[15] In a variation on this approach, in avatar therapy, a computerized representation of the voice, based on the voice hearer's description of it, is controlled by the therapist and used to facilitate a therapeutic dialogue.[16]

Notwithstanding the advances made in recent years, some have found the medical approach deeply unhelpful. An over-reliance on medication and professional-led treatments have often disempowered patients. The stigma associated with psychiatric diagnosis, and the perceived poor prognosis, have added to the distress directly attributable to the voices. In response to this, the Hearing Voices Movement seeks to empower voice hearers and promotes recovery rather than cure. Following a successful conference held in Holland in 1987, the first UK conference was held in Manchester in 1990. The Movement now has groups in 35 countries worldwide. Voice hearers are respected as experts-by-experience, and local groups provide mutual support.[17]

Within this array of options, spirituality and faith receive a variable, but usually minor, role. Thus, for example, Jack Jenner notes that

---

12 Moseley *et al.* (2015).

13 Hardy (2017); Thomas *et al.* (2014).

14 Thomas *et al.* (2014).

15 Corstens, Longden and May (2012).

16 Alderson-Day and Jones (2018).

17 See Corstens *et al.* (2014); Dillon and Hornstein (2013); Romme and Escher (1993); and Romme *et al.* (2009).

prayer and meditation may provide a coping resource that may be incorporated within the provisions of HIT.[18] Amy Hardy[19] acknowledges the developmental role that spirituality may play where childhood is associated both with strict religious observance and physical abuse. Within the Hearing Voices Movement, greater attention is given to the possibility that voices may convey positive spiritual or religious meaning, and attention is drawn to the apparently similar voice-hearing experiences of figures such as Jesus, Moses and Muhammad.[20] The narratives related by people in recovery give an account of how they have experienced, and managed, the relationship between faith and voice hearing.[21] This person-centred focus allows each voice hearer to find a way to integrate their experiences of their voices within their understanding of their faith, but does not offer any systematic account of how others may do this.

Pierre-Yves Brandt *et al.*,[22] studying patients with schizophrenia in Geneva and Québec, found that two-thirds identified spirituality or religion as important in coping with their illness, but that their clinicians were often unaware of this.[23] In an attempt to address this, they offered a training session, followed by individual religious supervision, to eight psychiatrists in Geneva. Attention was given to positive and negative methods of religious coping employed by the patients, liaison with chaplains and clergy, religious identity and values, differentiation of delusion from faith, and the relationship between psychiatry and faith. After three months it was found that patients maintained an interest in discussing religious matters with their psychiatrist, and were more likely to attend clinic appointments as compared with a control group. Sadly, and in contrast to this, the clinicians' motivation to discuss spirituality or religion decreased. Whilst there is no specific

18 Jenner (2016, pp.30, 70).

19 Hardy (2017).

20 See, for example, Romme and Escher (1993, pp.88–120).

21 See, for example, the stories of Caroline, Debra, Fernand, Mien and Ron in Romme *et al.* (2009).

22 Brandt *et al.* (2012).

23 Sixty-two per cent of patients in Geneva and 91 per cent in Québec identified as Christian.

reference in this publication to any discussions that were had between the psychiatrist and patient concerning voice hearing, this study does offer one model of how interventions might be constructed in order to improve attention to matters of spirituality or religion amongst those hearing voices in the context of psychosis.

Given the current interest in spiritually and religious integrated approaches to CBT in the treatment of affective (and other) disorders,[24] and the evidence for benefit of CBT in working with people who hear distressing voices, it is perhaps surprising that there does not, as yet, appear to be any published research on religiously integrated CBT for voices.

Clinical and pastoral responses to demonic voices

It is unlikely that most clinicians would treat demonic voices differently than other AVHs. Depending on the diagnosis, treatment options might include a wide range of possible pharmacological or psychological therapies. Whilst the hearing of demonic voices is not exactly the same thing as explanatory frameworks concerning demonic influence (for example, beliefs about possession), the two are clearly closely interrelated (see Chapter 13). The question of the possibility of possession arose for seven of the Christians whose stories are recorded in this book: Errol, Lucy, Willelmina, Dominic, Perpetua, Clare and Rachel. In each case, this possibility was considered based on the evil voices that they had heard, but only Errol explicitly described these voices as 'demons'.[25]

---

24 See, for example, Ebrahimi *et al.* (2013); Koenig *et al.* (2015); and Rosmarin *et al.* (2011).

25 Lucy described her evil voices as spirits. Willelmina understands her voices to be those of her ancestors. Dominic, after considering the possibility that the voice was demonic, concludes that it is an 'alter', a dissociated psychological part of his own identity. Perpetua describes her voices as the devil, or as devils. Clare refers to her voice primarily as 'the Voice', but this voice threatens her that she will come under the power of the devil if she does not obey it. Rachel refers to her voice as 'the voice', but comes to associate it with her abuser, and also considers the possibility that it might have been the voice of Satan.

David Enoch and Hadrian Ball succinctly state 'The treatment of possession syndromes is that of the underlying condition.'[26] In the series of 66 patients with possession syndrome studied by Pow-Meng Yap,[27] who received what would have been standard treatment at the time, all were discharged in remission, except for seven who were described as 'only partially remitted'. Two to five years later, of 41 patients who responded to follow-up, 33 were described as 'well' (meaning that they were free from symptoms and able to work) and 8 as 'unwell'. Unfortunately, in this mixed diagnostic group, it is not clear how many patients were hearing voices.

There is increasing awareness in psychiatry of the importance of taking into account cultural context, and there is a tension between the twin dangers of over-accommodating cultural and religious beliefs concerning the demonic and completely ignoring them.[28] Failure to provide appropriate medical treatment and injudicious endorsement of deliverance or exorcism may both be unhelpful and harmful. Getting the balance right is undoubtedly difficult for all psychiatrists, and the tension will be no less acute for Christian psychiatrists than for others. However, the place of exorcism in psychiatric practice is extremely controversial, and perhaps especially so amongst Christians from different theological traditions. Amongst the stories included in the present book, reference to exorcism is made only by Lucy (in comparing her experience to Mary Magdalene in the Bible), Perpetua and Clare.

In a careful study of 15 women with dissociative identity disorder,[29] 14 of whom were subjected to exorcism, Elizabeth Bowman[30] found that exorcism was experienced as both emotionally and spiritually traumatic and worsened the clinical condition for most women. Thirteen of the women had themselves thought that they were possessed, and the hearing of voices provided one of the reasons for

26 Enoch and Ball (2001, p.236).

27 Yap (1960).

28 See the helpful discussion by Littlewood (2004).

29 In the publication, the diagnosis is given as multiple personality disorder. Current diagnostic terminology for this condition would be dissociative identity disorder.

30 Bowman (1991).

this belief for nine of them. Nine of the women had to be admitted to hospital as a result of the exorcism. In a study of seven patients with the same diagnosis, George Fraser,[31] in a similar study, also found that all patients experienced negative effects as a result of exorcism. However, in a later study by Dennis Bull, Joan Ellason and Colin Ross,[32] outcomes were polarized between positive and negative outcomes. They identified eight factors concerned with consent, cooperation and non-coercion of patients, which they believed discriminated between the good and bad outcome groups in their own study, and also used these factors to explain the different findings that they obtained compared with previous studies.

Suggestions that exorcism is effective as a treatment of schizophrenia, or other disorders, appear to be based largely or entirely on anecdotal evidence,[33] but this works both ways. Reports that this is helpful must be balanced against those that suggest that it is harmful. It was not helpful for Perpetua, and it was helpful to Clare only insofar as it reassured her that it was not what was needed (Chapter 11). Case reports compiled by those who are not medically qualified seem generally more optimistic than those by medically qualified authors, and in particular psychiatrists, but there are exceptions.[34] Even M. Scott Peck (1990), a psychiatrist whose popular report of two exorcisms is

31 Fraser (1993).

32 Bull, Ellason and Ross (1998).

33 See, for example Betty (2005); Irmak (2014); and McAll (1971).

34 Kiraly (1975) reports an interesting case of *folie à deux*, in which a mother and daughter both believed they were possessed and were hearing voices. Exorcism appears not to have been attempted, but the mother and daughter both responded well to psychiatric treatment. Pfeifer (1994) (case vignette 3) reports a case of borderline personality disorder attributed to demons, not helped by exorcism, culminating in a serious suicide attempt. Tajima-Pozo *et al.* (2011) report a case of schizophrenia in which priests persuaded a woman hearing voices that she was possessed. Repeated attempts at exorcism disrupted treatment and were ineffective. Maniam (1987) (case 2) reports a case of a man in Malaysia diagnosed as suffering from schizophrenia who had AVHs of the devil. Antipsychotic medication did not produce any amelioration of the voices, but a Christian exorcism was almost immediately, and dramatically, effective. The man discontinued all medication and remained well a year later.

cited approvingly as evidence of the effectiveness of exorcism,[35] is himself much more cautious:

> While I have endeavoured to my utmost to be objective, the fact remains that the preceding account of two cases of possession and exorcism is a subjective one of my personal experience.[36]

As discussed in Chapter 13, Chris MacKenna,[37] an Anglican priest, Jungian analyst and diocesan advisor on deliverance ministry with many years' experience, has argued on the basis of a series of case studies that a multiprofessional and multidisciplinary approach is almost always required in practice, and this has now been recognized as an essential basis of good practice in mainstream Christian denominations. The following discussion is concerned mainly with the Church of England,[38] but similar considerations apply in other denominational contexts.

In the absence of systematic outcome studies,[39] there must remain some doubt as to whether, or when, exorcism is effective and to what extent it causes harm. A small number of high-profile cases have, in the past, brought adverse publicity,[40] and, in response to these, policy and practice have been reviewed.

In a 1972 report of the Commission on Exorcism, convened by the Bishop of Exeter, exorcism was defined in theological terms:

> Christian exorcism is the binding of evil powers by the triumph of Christ Jesus, through the application of the power demonstrated by that triumph, in and by his Church.[41]

---

35 See, for example, Betty (2005).

36 Peck (1990, p.229).

37 MacKenna (2013).

38 For a history of exorcism within the Church of England, see Young (2018). An account of deliverance and exorcism in the 20th century in charismatic and evangelical churches more widely is provided by Collins (2011). For a more global perspective on practices in Pentecostal churches outside the Western world, see Anderson (2011).

39 Rosik (1997).

40 Milner (2010); Young (2018, pp.142–146).

41 Petitpierre (1972, p.16).

Both this report and the wider literature, lack the kind of critical, in-depth, interdisciplinary analysis that one might have hoped for in support of an understanding of exactly what this means in psychological and medical terms. However, very helpfully, the report goes on to give priority of attention to medical assessment and treatment in practice:

> In the first place it should be assumed that the patient's illness has a physical or mental cause, and the case should be referred by his general practitioner to a competent physician in psychological medicine. The exorcism of a person must not be performed until possible mental or physical illness has been excluded in this way...[42]

Should an exorcism still be thought to be indicated, it is made clear that this should only be undertaken with the explicit permission of the bishop, and by a person duly approved by him. The report cautions that failure of medical treatment should not be taken as an indication that the problem is a spiritual one, and success should not be taken as excluding this possibility. 'The diagnosis of demonic "possession" must rest on precise and positive criteria.'[43] Unfortunately, it is not made clear what these criteria are. There is no mention of demonic voices.

The 2012 revision of these guidelines reaffirms the advice that they offer, and re-emphasizes the need for a multidisciplinary approach involving healthcare professionals as well as suitably trained and supervised clergy, counsellors and therapists.[44] There is still no mention of demonic voices.

Some writers on this topic distinguish between 'deliverance' and exorcism.[45] The former, although not necessarily consistently defined, seems generally to be understood as something usually less invasive but broader in scope. Deliverance seems to involve prayer, confession, repentance and wider attention to healing of the whole person. It somewhat blurs the boundaries between the spiritual and the

---

42 Petitpierre (1972, p.23).

43 Petitpierre (1972, p.24).

44 At the time of writing, these guidelines are currently in the process of further review.

45 See, for example, Richards (1974).

psychological.[46] Exorcism might be understood as one option falling within the broader scope of deliverance, but only as the exception rather than the rule. However, it is not clear that 'deliverance ministry', in any of its various forms, might be any less potentially unhelpful to someone hearing demonic voices than would exorcism.

Taking into account all of the foregoing discussion, we are left with a frustrating lack of scientific evidence, and a bewildering diversity of theological opinion and pastoral practice. Overall, exorcism would not generally appear to be a helpful intervention for people hearing demonic voices. Indeed, it may often be harmful, especially where there is a diagnosable psychiatric disorder. The one thing that is completely clear is that exorcism should never be embarked on as a pastoral response to the hearing of demonic voices without first involving mental health professionals in assessment and planning of care. Where the mental health professionals concerned are Christians, they need to be careful to observe proper professional boundaries and adhere to good practice, as outlined by the Royal College of Psychiatrists and the General Medical Council.[47] Given that exorcism is a potentially harmful intervention, and something about which different Christians hold different views, the role of the Christian professional is to advocate for their patient, and not to pursue their own theological agenda.

To conclude this section, it must be observed that, in practice, people who hear demonic voices are encountered both within mental health services and within the ministry of the Christian churches. Each needs to be aware of what the other has to offer, and there are potential harms associated, both with failing to provide spiritual care within mental health services and also with failing to identify and refer for treatment those within the churches who are suffering from mental disorders. Arguably, the failure to identify and treat mental illness is likely to be the cause of greater harm, and the emphasis on multiprofessional working adopted by the Church of England (and other Christian churches) is therefore to be welcomed.

46 Milner (2010).

47 Royal College of Psychiatrists (2009); General Medical Council (2013a).

Spiritually significant voices in clinical and pastoral practice

It is important to reiterate that many Christians hearing spiritually significant voices do not need clinical or pastoral help. However, where these voices are distressing, confusing or difficult to make sense of, they may become the occasion for discussion during clinical care, or in the course of a pastoral conversation. The critical issue for clinical consideration will be whether or not pharmacological or psychological interventions might be beneficial, either to reduce the distress associated with the voices, or to reduce the frequency of the voices. The nature of such interventions, if needed at all, will be influenced by the underlying diagnosis. However, it is important to dispel any illusion that a psychiatric diagnosis precludes a spiritually significant experience. Meaning making is just as important in the context of illness as it is in the context of health.

Pastoral care will always be concerned with facilitating this process of meaning making. Sometimes it will engage with difficult questions of discernment. Is this voice demonic, or divine? Does it reflect primarily the conscious or unconscious mental concerns of the person hearing it? If the voice is demonic, does it indicate the need for deliverance ministry? Although I have explored this question at some length in this chapter, I expect it to be the least frequently important one to address in practice. I strongly suspect that demonic voices will most often be seen by psychiatrists – including Christian psychiatrists – as evidence of mental disorder. Demonic voices are not represented by most theologians or practitioners as being consistently occurring evidence of possession. However, descriptions of people believed to be possessed do sometimes include reference to them. In the stories included in the earlier chapters of this book, such voices always raised the question. The possibility that they indicate a state of possession may therefore often be a concern of those who are unfortunate enough to hear them. The question of what they mean, and how to handle them, is thus an important one when it arises.

It is now clear that the hearing of voices should not be taken as invariable evidence of mental disorder. Indeed, in the Christian context which has been the primary focus of this book, that would seem to be the exception rather than the rule. The mystery of whether and when and how God speaks through such voices should probably be allowed to remain just that – mysterious. It is not helpful to explain such things away. It is important to search for meaning. Christians hearing spiritually significant voices have important, fascinating and meaningful stories to tell. The good clinician, and the good pastor, are able to facilitate the telling of these stories and the meaning making with which they are associated.

References

Alderson-Day, B. and Jones, N. (2018) 'Understanding avatar therapy: Who, or what, is changing?' *The Lancet Psychiatry 5*, 2–3.

Anderson, A. (2011) 'Deliverance and Exorcism in Majority World Pentecostalism.' In W.K. Kay and R. Parry (eds) *Exorcism and Deliverance: Multi-Disciplinary Studies* (pp.101–119). Milton Keynes: Paternoster.

Asgeirsdottir, G.H., Sigurbjornsson, E., Traustadottir, R., Sigurdardottir, V., Gunnarsdottir, S. and Kelly, E. (2013) '"To cherish each day as it comes": A qualitative study of spirituality among persons receiving palliative care.' *Support Care Cancer 21*, 1445–1451.

Barbour, I. (2002) *Nature, Human Nature, and God*. London: SPCK.

Barrett, T.R. and Etheridge, J.B. (1992) 'Verbal hallucinations in normals, I: People who hear "voices".' *Applied Cognitive Psychology 6*, 379–387.

Barton, S.C. (2008) 'Thinking about demons and the demonic.' *Theology 111*, 83–92.

Betty, S. (2005) 'The growing evidence for "demonic possession": What should psychiatry's response be?' *Journal of Religion and Health 14*, 13–30.

Blom, J.D. and Hoffer, C.B.M. (2012) 'Djinns.' In J.D. Blom and I.E.C. Sommer (eds) *Hallucinations: Research and Practice* (pp. 235–247). New York: Springer.

Bomford, R. (1999) *The Symmetry of God*. London: Free Association.

Bowman, E.S. (1991) 'Clinical and spiritual effects of exorcism in fifteen patients with multiple personality disorder.' *Dissociation VI*, 222–238.

Brandt, P.-Y., Mohr, S., Gillièron, C., Rieben, I. and Huguelet, P. (2012) 'Religious coping in schizophrenia patients: Spiritual support in medical care and pastoral counselling.' *Toronto Journal of Theology 28*, 193–207.

Bull, D.L., Ellason, J.W. and Ross, C.A. (1998) 'Exorcism revisited: Positive outcomes with dissociative identity disorder.' *Journal of Psychology and Theology 26*, 188–196.

Cassaniti, J.L. and Luhrmann, T.M. (2014) 'The cultural kindling of spiritual experiences.' *Current Anthropology 55*, S333–S343.

Coles, R. (1990) *The Spiritual Life of Children*. Boston, MA: Houghton Mifflin.

Colledge, E., Walsh, J. and Leclercq, J. (eds) (1977) *Julian of Norwich: Showings*. New York: Paulist.

Collins, J. (2011) 'Deliverance and Exorcism in the Twentieth Century.' In W.K. Kay and R. Parry (eds) *Exorcism and Deliverance: Multi-Disciplinary Studies* (pp.86–100). Milton Keynes: Paternoster.

Cook, C.C.H. (2011a) 'The faith of the psychiatrist.' *Mental Health, Religion & Culture 14*, 9–17.

Cook, C.C.H. (2011b) *The Philokalia and the Inner Life: On Passions and Prayer*. Cambridge: James Clarke.

Cook, C.C.H. (2013a) 'Controversies on the Place of Spirituality and Religion in Psychiatric Practice.' In C.C.H. Cook (ed.) *Spirituality, Theology and Mental Health* (pp.1–19). London, SCM.

Cook, C.C.H. (2013b) *Recommendations for Psychiatrists on Spirituality and Religion*. London: Royal College of Psychiatrists.

Cook, C.C.H. (2015) 'Religious psychopathology: The prevalence of religious content of delusions and hallucinations in mental disorder.' *International Journal of Social Psychiatry 61*, 404–425.

Cook, C.C.H. (2017a) 'Speak, Lord: Thy servant heareth.' *Church Times 17*, 21 April.

Cook, C.C.H. (2017b) 'Learning to discern.' *Church Times 17*, 28 April.

Cook, C.C.H. (2017c) 'Voices immanent and transcendent.' *Church Times 17*, 5 May.

Cook, C.C.H. (2017d) 'Spirituality and religion in psychiatry: The impact of policy.' *Mental Health, Religion & Culture 20*, 589–594.

Cook, C.C.H. (2018) *Hearing Voices, Demonic and Divine: Scientific and Theological Perspectives*. London: Routledge. Available for free download: http://dro.dur.ac.uk/27003.

Corstens, D., Longden, E. and May, R. (2012) 'Talking with voices: Exploring what is expressed by the voices people hear.' *Psychosis 4*, 95–104.

Corstens, D., Longden, E., Mccarthy-Jones, S., Waddingham, R. and Thomas, N. (2014) 'Emerging perspectives from the Hearing Voices Movement: Implications for research and practice.' *Schizophrenia Bulletin 40*, Suppl. 4, S285–S294.

Corstens, D., Longden, E., Rydinger, B., Bentall, R. and Os, J.V. (2013) 'Treatment of hallucinations: A comment.' *Psychosis 5*, 98–102.

Cottam, S., Paul, S.N., Doughty, O.J., Carpenter, L., *et al.* (2011) 'Does religious belief enable positive interpretation of auditory hallucinations? A comparison of religious voice hearers with and without psychosis.' *Cognitive Neuropsychiatry 16*, 403–421.

Cunningham, L. and Rogers, J. (1984) *Is That Really You, God? Hearing the Voice of God*. Monroe, WA: Youth With a Mission (YWAM).

Daalman, K., Diederen, K.M., Derks, E.M., van Lutterveld, R., Kahn, R.S. and Sommer, I.E. (2012) 'Childhood trauma and auditory verbal hallucinations.' *Psychological Medicine 42*, 2475–2484.

David, A.S. (2004) 'The cognitive neuropsychiatry of auditory verbal hallucinations: An overview.' *Cognitive Neuropsychiatry 9*, 107–123.

Davies, M.F., Griffin, M. and Vice, S. (2001) 'Affective reactions to auditory hallucinations in psychotic, evangelical and control groups.' *British Journal of Clinical Psychology 40*, 361–370.

Davies, S. (2014) *Spirit Possession and the Origins of Christianity*. Dublin: Bardic Press.

Davis, P.E., Meins, E. and Fernyhough, C. (2013) 'Individual differences in children's private speech: The role of imaginary companions.' *Journal of Experimental Child Psychology 116*, 561–571.

Dein, S. and Cook, C.C.H. (2015) 'God put a thought into my mind: The charismatic Christian experience of receiving communications from God.' *Mental Health, Religion & Culture* 1–17.

Dein, S. and Illaiee, A.S. (2013) 'Jinn and mental health: Looking at Jinn possession in modern psychiatric practice.' *The Psychiatrist 37*, 290–293.

Dein, S. and Littlewood, R. (2007) 'The voice of God.' *Anthropology & Medicine 14*, 213–228.

Dennett, D.C. (1991) *Consciousness Explained*. London: Penguin.

Dillon, J. and Hornstein, G.A. (2013) 'Hearing voices peer support groups: A powerful alternative for people in distress.' *Psychosis 5*, 286–295.

Dow, G. (1980) 'The case for the existence of demons.' *Churchman 94*, 199–208.

Dunn, J.D.G. and Twelftree, G.H. (1980) 'Demon-possession and exorcism in the New Testament.' *Churchman 94*, 210–225.

Ebrahimi, A., Neshatdoost, H.T., Mousavi, S.G., Asadollahi, G.A. and Nasiri, H. (2013) 'Controlled randomized clinical trial of spirituality integrated psychotherapy, cognitive-behavioral therapy and medication intervention on depressive symptoms and dysfunctional attitudes in patients with dysthymic disorder.' *Advanced Biomedical Research 2*, 53.

Enoch, M.D. and Ball, H.N. (2001) *Uncommon Psychiatric Syndromes*. London: Arnold.

Esquirol, J.E.D. (1845) *Mental Maladies: A Treatise on Insanity*. New York: Hafner.

Fernyhough, C. (2016) *The Voices Within: The History and Science of How We Talk to Ourselves.* London: Profile.

Fraser, G.A. (1993) 'Exorcism rituals: Effects on multiple personality disorder patients.' *Dissociation VI*, 239–244.

General Medical Council (2013a) *Good Medical Practice.* London: General Medical Council.

General Medical Council (2013b) *Personal Beliefs and Medical Practice.* London: General Medical Council.

Goff, D.C., Brotman, A.W., Kindlon, D., Waites, M. and Amico, E. (1991) 'The delusion of possession in chronically psychotic patients.' *The Journal of Nervous & Mental Disease 179*, 567–571.

Hardy, A. (2017) 'Pathways from trauma to psychotic experiences: A theoretically informed model of posttraumatic stress in psychosis.' *Frontiers in Psychology 8*, 697.

Hartog, K. and Gow, K.M. (2005) 'Religious attributions pertaining to the causes and cures of mental illness.' *Mental Health, Religion & Culture 8*, 263–276.

Hick, J. (2010) *The New Frontier of Religion and Science: Religious Experience, Neuroscience and the Transcendent.* Basingstoke: Palgrave Macmillan.

House of Bishops of the Church of England (2019) *Parish Safeguarding Handbook.* London: Church House Publishing.

Huggett, J. (1986) *Listening to God.* London: Hodder & Stoughton.

Huggett, J. (1990) 'Why Ignatian spirituality hooks Protestants.' *The Way* 22–34.

Irmak, M.K. (2014) 'Schizophrenia or possession?' *Journal of Religion & Health 53*, 773–777.

Isaacs, T.C. (1987) 'The possessive states disorder: The diagnosis of demonic possession.' *Pastoral Psychology 35*, 263–273.

Israel, M. (1997) *Exorcism: The Removal of Evil Influences.* London: SPCK.

Ivens, M. and Hughes, G.W. (eds) (2004) *The Spiritual Exercises of Saint Ignatius of Loyola.* Leominster: Gracewing.

Ivens, M. and Munitiz, J.A. (2007) *Keeping in Touch: Posthumous Papers on Ignatian Topics.* Leominster: Gracewing.

Iyadurai, J. (2015) *Transformative Religious Experience: A Phenomenological Understanding of Religious Conversion.* Eugene, OR: Pickwick.

James, W. (1902) *The Varieties of Religious Experience: A Study in Human Nature.* New York: Longmans, Green & Co.

Jenner, J.A. (2016) *Hallucination-focused Integrative Therapy: A Specific Treatment that Hits Auditory Verbal Hallucinations.* London: Routledge.

Johns, L.C., Kompus, K., Connell, M., Humpston, C., *et al.* (2014) 'Auditory verbal hallucinations in persons with and without a need for care.' *Schizophrenia Bulletin 40*, Suppl. 4, S255–S264.

Jung, C.G. (1983) *Memories, Dreams, Reflections.* Glasgow: Flamingo.

Karanci, A.N. (2014) 'Concerns about schizophrenia or possession?' *Journal of Religion and Health 53*, 1691–1692.

Kavanaugh, K. and Rodriguez, O. (1991) *The Collected Works of St John of the Cross.* Washington, DC: Institute of Carmelite Studies.

Kemp, S. and Williams, K. (1987) 'Demonic possession and mental disorder in medieval and early modern Europe.' *Psychological Medicine 17*, 21–29.

Kent, G. and Wahass, S. (1996) 'The content and characteristics of auditory hallucinations in Saudi Arabia and the UK: A cross-cultural comparison.' *Acta Psychiatrica Scandinavica 94*, 433–437.

Kiraly, S.J. (1975) 'Folie à deux: A case of "demonic possession" involving mother and daughter.' *Canadian Psychiatric Association Journal 20*, 223–227.

Koch, K. (1971) *Occult Bondage and Deliverance.* Grand Rapids, MI: Kregel.

Koenig, H.G., Pearce, M.J., Nelson, B., Shaw, S.F., *et al.* (2015) 'Religious vs. conventional cognitive behavioral therapy for major depression in persons with chronic medical illness. A pilot randomized trial.' *Journal of Nervous & Mental Disease 203*, 243–251.

Kolodiejchuk, B. (2007) *Mother Teresa: Come Be My Light.* London: Rider.

Kübler-Ross, E. (1998) *The Wheel of Life: A Memoir of Living and Dying.* New York: Simon & Schuster.

Leff, J. (1975) '"Exotic" treatments and Western psychiatry.' *Psychological Medicine* 5, 125–128.

Lhermitte, J. (1963) *Diabolical Possession, True and False.* London: Burns & Oates.

Litchfield, K. (2006) *Tend My Flock: Sustaining Good Pastoral Care.* Norwich: Canterbury Press.

Littlewood, R. (2004) 'Possession states.' *Psychiatry* 3, 8–10.

Louth, A. (2004) 'The Literature of the Monastic Movement.' In F. Young, L. Ayres and A. Louth (eds) *The Cambridge History of Early Christian Literature* (pp.373–381). Cambridge: Cambridge University Press.

Luhrmann, T.M. (2005) 'The art of hearing God: Absorption, dissociation, and contemporary American spirituality.' *Spiritus* 5, 133–157.

Luhrmann, T.M. (2012) *When God Talks Back.* New York: Knopf.

Luhrmann, T.M. (2017) 'Diversity within the psychotic continuum.' *Schizophrenia Bulletin* 43, 27–31.

Luhrmann, T.M., Nusbaum, H. and Thisted, R. (2013) '"Lord, teach us to pray": Prayer practice affects cognitive processing.' *Journal of Cognition and Culture* 13, 159–177.

MacKenna, C. (2013) 'Exorcism: Some Theological, Psychoanalytic and Cultural Reflections on the Practice of Christian Deliverance Ministry in the Light of Clinical and Pastoral Experience.' In C.C.H. Cook (ed.) *Spirituality, Theology & Mental Health* (pp.75–93). London: SCM Press.

Machery, E. (2018) 'Know Thyself: Beliefs vs. Desires in Inner Speech.' In P. Langland-Hassan and A. Vicente (eds) *Inner Speech: New Voices* (pp.261–275). Oxford: Oxford University Press.

Maniam, T. (1987) 'Exorcism and psychiatric illness: Two case reports.' *Medical Journal of Malaysia 42*, 317–319.

Maslow, A.H. (1964) *Religions, Values and Peak-Experiences.* London: Penguin.

McAll, R.K. (1971) 'Demonosis or the possession syndrome.' *International Journal of Social Psychiatry 17*, 150–158.

McCarthy-Jones, S. (2012) *Hearing Voices: The Histories, Causes and Meanings of Auditory Verbal Hallucinations.* Cambridge: Cambridge University Press.

McKane, W. (1995) *A Late Harvest: Reflections on the Old Testament.* Edinburgh: T&T Clark.

Millham, A. and Easton, S. (1998) 'Prevalence of auditory hallucinations in nurses in mental health.' *Journal of Psychiatric and Mental Health Nursing* 5, 95–99.

Milner, N. (2010) 'Giving the devil his due process: Exorcism in the Church of England.' *Journal of Contemporary Religion* 15, 247–272.

Moberly, R.W.L. (2006) *Prophecy and Discernment.* Cambridge: Cambridge University Press.

Montgomery, J.W. (1976) *Demon Possession.* Minneapolis, MN: Bethany House.

Morin, A. (2018) 'The Self-Reflective Functions of Inner Speech: Thirteen Years Later.' In P. Langland-Hassan and A. Vicente (eds) *Inner Speech: New Voices* (pp.276–298). Oxford: Oxford University Press.

Moseley, P., Alderson-Day, B., Ellison, A., Jardri, R. and Fernyhough, C. (2015) 'Non-invasive brain stimulation and auditory verbal hallucinations: New techniques and future directions.' *Frontiers in Neuroscience* 9, 515, 1–12.

Oesterreich, T.K. (1930) *Possession Demoniacal and Other among Primitive Races, in Antiquity, the Middle Ages, and Modern Times.* Alcester: Thomson Press.

Peck, M.S. (1990) *People of the Lie.* London: Arrow.

Peck, M.S. (2005) *Glimpses of the Devil: A Psychiatrist's Personal Account of Possession, Exorcism and Redemption*. New York: Free Press.

Perry, M. (1996) *Deliverance*. London: SPCK.

Peters, E., Ward, T., Jackson, M., Woodruff, P., *et al.* (2017) 'Clinical relevance of appraisals of persistent psychotic experiences in people with and without a need for care: An experimental study.' *The Lancet Psychiatry 4*, 927–936.

Petitpierre, D.R. (ed.) (1972) *Exorcism: The Report of a Commission Convened by the Bishop of Exeter*. London: SPCK.

Pfeifer, S. (1994) 'Belief in demons and exorcism in psychiatric patients in Switzerland.' *British Journal of Medical Psychology 67*, 247–258.

Pine-Coffin, R.S. (1961) *Saint Augustine: Confessions*. Harmondsworth: Penguin.

Polkinghorne, J. (1998) *Science and Theology: An Introduction*. London: SPCK.

Poole, R. and Cook, C.C.H. (2011) 'Praying with a patient constitutes a breach of professional boundaries in psychiatric practice.' *British Journal of Psychiatry 199*, 94–98.

Poole, R., Cook, C.C.H. and Higgo, R. (2019) 'Psychiatrists, spirituality and religion.' *British Journal of Psychiatry 214*, 181–182.

Posey, T.B. and Losch, M.E. (1983) 'Auditory hallucinations of hearing voices in 375 normal subjects.' *Imagination, Cognition and Personality 3*, 99–113.

Praying Medic (ed.) (2017) *God Speaks: Perspectives on Hearing God's Voice*, Gilbert, AZ: Inkity Press.

Puchalski, C., Ferrell, B., Virani, R., Otis-Green, S., *et al.* (2009) 'Improving the quality of spiritual care as a dimension of palliative care: The report of the Consensus Conference.' *Journal of Palliative Care 12*, 885–904.

Pytches, D. (1989) *Does God Speak Today?* London: Hodder & Stoughton.

Reinders, A.A. (2008) 'Cross-examining dissociative identity disorder: Neuroimaging and etiology on trial.' *Neurocase 14*, 44–53.

Richards, J. (1974) *But Deliver Us from Evil: An Introduction to the Demonic Dimension in Pastoral Care*. London: DLT.

Romme, M. and Escher, S. (eds) (1993) *Accepting Voices*. London: Mind.

Romme, M., Escher, S., Dillon, J., Corstens, D. and Morris, M. (2009) *Living with Voices: 50 Stories of Recovery*. Ross on Wye: PCCS.

Rosik, C.H. (1997) 'When discernment fails: The case for outcome studies on exorcism.' *Journal of Psychology and Theology 25*, 354–363.

Rosmarin, D.H., Auerbach, R.P., Bigda-Peyton, J.S., Björgvinsson, T. and Levendusky, P.G. (2011) 'Integrating spirituality into cognitive behavioral therapy in an acute psychiatric setting: A pilot study.' *Journal of Cognitive Psychotherapy 25*, 287–303.

Royal College of Psychiatrists (2009) *Good Psychiatric Practice*. London: Royal College of Psychiatrists.

Royal College of Psychiatrists (2018) *Person-Centred Care: Implications for Training in Psychiatry*. London: Royal College of Psychiatrists.

Sall, M.J. (1976) 'Demon possession or psychopathology? A clinical differentiation.' *Journal of Psychology and Theology 4*, 286–290.

Schendel, E. and Kourany, R.-F.C. (1980) 'Cacodemonomania and exorcism in children.' *Journal of Clinical Psychiatry 41*, 119–123.

Scrutton, A.P. (2015) 'Schizophrenia or possession? A reply to Kemal Irmak and Nuray Karanci.' *Journal of Religion & Health 54*, 1963–1968.

Sheldrake, P. (ed.) (1991) *The Way of Ignatius Loyola: Contemporary Approaches to the Spiritual Exercises*. London: SPCK.

Sheldrake, P. (1998) *Befriending Our Desires*. London: DLT.

Sherley-Price, L. (1952) *Thomas à Kempis: The Imitation of Christ*. Harmondsworth: Penguin.

Sherley-Price, L. (1988) *The Ladder of Perfection*. London: Penguin.

Silf, M. (1998) *Landmarks: An Ignatian Journey*. London: DLT.

Silf, M. (2004) *Companions of Christ: Ignatian Spirituality for Everyday Living*. Norwich: Canterbury Press.

Slade, P.D. and Bentall, R.P. (1988) *Sensory Deception: A Scientific Analysis of Hallucination*. London: Croom Helm.

Sommer, I.E., Slotema, C.W., Daskalakis, Z.J., Derks, E.M., Blom, J.D. and van der Gaag, M. (2012) 'The treatment of hallucinations in schizophrenia spectrum disorders.' *Schizophrenia Bulletin 38*, 704–714.

Spanos, N.P. and Moretti, P. (1988) 'Correlates of mystical and diabolical experiences in a sample of female university students.' *Journal for the Scientific Study of Religion 27*, 105–116.

Starbuck, E.D. (1901) *The Psychology of Religion: An Empirical Study of the Growth of Religious Consciousness*. London: Walter Scott.

Streeter, B.H. and Appasamy, A.J. (1926) *The Sadhu: A Study in Mysticism and Practical Religion*. London: Macmillan.

Tajima-Pozo, K., Zambrano-Enriquez, D., de Anta, L., Moron, M.D., *et al.* (2011) 'Practicing exorcism in schizophrenia.' *BMJ Case Reports 2011*, 1–3.

Talbot, S. (1986) *The Confessions of a Reluctant Mystic: The Search for the Hidden Christ in an Ordinary Life*. Basingstoke: Marsall Pickering.

Thomas, N., Hayward, M., Peters, E., van der Gaag, M., *et al.* (2014) 'Psychological therapies for auditory hallucinations (voices): Current status and key directions for future research.' *Schizophrenia Bulletin 40*, Suppl. 4, S202–S212.

Watts, F. (2007) 'Personal Transformation.' In F. Watts (ed.) *Jesus and Psychology* (pp.62–77). London: Darton, Longman & Todd.

Weil, S. (1952) *Gravity and Grace*. London: Routledge & Kegan Paul.

Whitwell, F.D. and Barker, M.G. (1980) '"Possession" in psychiatric patients in Britain.' *British Journal of Medical Psychology 53*, 287–295.

Wilkinson, S. and Fernyhough, C. (2018) 'When Inner Speech Misleads.' In P. Langland-Hassan and A. Vicente (eds) *Inner Speech: New Voices* (pp.244–260). Oxford: Oxford University Press.

Willard, D. (1999) *Hearing God: Building an Intimate Relationship with the Creator*. London: Fount.

Williamson, S.C. (2016) *Hearing God in Conversation: How to Recognise His Voice Everywhere*. Grand Rapids, MI: Kregel.

Wilson, M. (1975) 'Exorcism: A clinical/pastoral practice which raises serious questions.' *Expository Times 86*, 292–295.

Wright, N. (2011) 'Deliverance and exorcism in theological perspective 1: Is there any substance to evil?' In M. Cartledge, N. Hudson and K. Warrington (eds) *Exorcism and Deliverance: Multi-Disciplinary Studies* (pp.203–221). Milton Keynes: Paternoster.

Yap, P.M. (1960) 'The possession syndrome: A comparison of Hong Kong and French findings.' *Journal of Mental Science 106*, 114–137.

Young, F. (2018) *A History of Anglican Exorcism: Deliverance and Demonology in Church Ritual*. London: I.B. Tauris.